Learning Anew

Final Report of the
Research and Development Project

Teaching and Learning for the 21st Century, 2003-07

A school-university initiative by the Education Department, NUI
Maynooth and fifteen post-primary schools in Leinster

Pádraig Hogan, Anne Brosnan, Bernadette de Róiste, Alec
MacAlister, Anthony Malone, Nigel Quirke-Bolt, Greg Smith

Preface by John Coolahan

Education Department, NUI Maynooth 2007

Acknowledgements

The TL21 project is grateful to The Atlantic Philanthropies, the chief funders of the project; also to the Department of Education and Science for supplementary funding and to the National University of Ireland, Maynooth for making facilities available. A particular word of thanks is due to the International Consultative Panel and to the National Advisory Committee. The names of the members of these two bodies are provided in the appendices.

CONTENTS

Preface

'Teaching and Learning for the 21ˢᵗ Century (TL21)' is the title of a four-year, multi-layered research and development project conducted by the Education Department of NUI Maynooth in conjunction with clusters of post-primary schools in three regions of Leinster (2003-2007). *Learning Anew* is the final report on that project, prepared by the project leader, Dr. Pádraig Hogan and project team members. The report is a valuable contribution to the small, but growing body of research literature located within Irish educational policy paradigms and school circumstances. One of the great virtues of *Learning Anew* is the jargon-free style in which it is written. School leaders and teachers will readily relate to the authors' treatment of the issues and contexts. The report is a succinct, focused and direct account and analysis of issues involved in, and arising from the project. In a sense, the report might best be viewed as a handbook for action towards qualitative improvement in teaching and learning, which are the core purposes of schools. *Learning Anew* conveys many ideas, suggestions and examples which invite a 'can do' or applied approach by educational practitioners.

The participating Principals, Deputy Principals and teachers deserve great credit for the time and effort put in by them. However, on the evidence reported here one considers that they gained a great deal from their involvement. Whole-hearted engagement with well-designed continuing professional development activity can be a catalyst that unleashes new energies, fosters fresh enthusiasm, cultivates deeper understanding and fine-hones pedagogic skills. The nature of the teaching career requires such re-invigoration on a periodic basis. This type of activity is at the heart of being a reflective practitioner.

One of the most striking features revealed by the report is the extent of partnership that pervaded the project. While Atlantic Philanthropies were the valued main funders, the Department of Education and Science also provided resources and took an active professional partnership role in support of the project. Teacher unions and management bodies were professionally interested in,

i

and supportive of the project. Some of the post-primary in-career support agencies engaged actively with the TL21 team. Partnership was also in evidence by the support of members of the Advisory Committee and advice from the distinguished International Consultative Panel. However, partnership was most directly present in the very innovative forms of relationship which emerged between the university staff and the school personnel. This took place in the schools, in the university, in Education Centres and in a variety of other regional locations.

The project's seminars, workshops, exhibitions, colloquia and video productions all provided rich opportunities for learning from one another – leaning anew – in a supportive and encouraging context. While the report cannot capture the atmosphere and collegial spirit that prevailed on such occasions, sometimes facilitated by an overnight stay, the report's content does testify to the richness of the questioning, the dialogue, the experimentation, the guidance, the exchange of experiences that took place between participants. The project provided the supportive framework and stimulus for fresh thinking and action on curricular and pedagogic issues of direct import to classroom processes. A pattern of professional collegiality prevailed, and was particularly evident n the 'critical friend' dimension.

The school leaders and teachers were particularly focused on creating favourable teaching and learning environments, and on designing styles of pedagogy on best practice lines. Another key concern of the project was to nurture students to be active and responsible participants in their own learning, thereby lessening the tradition of dependency and relatively passive engagement that sometimes prevails. The sections of the report dealing with this dimension, and particularly Chapter 4, which features many student voices, make fascinating reading. The hope is that the skills and attitudes cultivated by the students will stand them in good stead in an era of lifelong learning. As with the case with the interim report on the project, *Voices from School* (2005), the views of teachers and students enrich this document.

The cultivation of instructional leadership in schools was a core element of the TL21 project, and the Principals and Deputy Principals who participated explored many of the constraining feature of contemporary schools which tend to inhibit the exercise of such leadership. Successful efforts were made by many of the school leaders to create more space and opportunity to focus purposely and decisively on quality-of-learning issues in the schools. Valuable inputs were made by some of the foremost international thinkers and researchers in the field of school leadership, including members of the project's International Consultative Panel.

The TL21 project also allowed for those teachers interested in doing so to utilise their engagement with the project as a means to proceed to academic accreditation at Post-Graduate Diploma or Master's Degree level. This was done through action research studies and involved the university in exploring new ways of processing the work of post-graduate students. The in-depth studies of the accreditation participants should be of major benefit to them as promoters of qualitative teaching and learning in their schools.

While directly benefiting the schools involved, the TL21 project seeks, as a research and development exercise firmly rooted in the day-to-day circumstances of Irish schools, to inform policy and practice at national level to help position Irish schooling for the challenges of the 'knowledge society'. The focus of the project is on one of the key challenges facing Irish education – improving the quality of teaching and learning. The project's efforts have been very much in line with best international practice and has incorporated much of the most advanced thinking on re-shaping the work of schools to meet new social, cultural, economic and educational circumstances. The project has rightly empha-sised that teachers need to be in the vanguard of lifelong learners, especially as their styles of teaching have a huge influence on whether their student will be equipped to be lifelong learners into the future.

This report correctly identifies the continuing professional development of teachers as an issue which should be a central matter in national development planning if Ireland is to achieve its potential development within the knowledge society. The suggestions for policy and practice provide valuable insights for policy makers. If Ireland is to make a qualitative leap forward in curricular and pedagogic policy implementation, which it needs to do, then close attention should be paid to the suggestions in the final chapter of this report.

The work of all those involved in the project should be greatly commended, not least for re-establishing joy at the heart of the teaching and learning process.

John Coolahan
Chair, Advisory Committee
December 2007

Introduction

The TL21 project (*Teaching and Learning for the 21ˢᵗ Century* 2003-2007) is a research and development initiative for innovative teaching and learning that has been organised by the Education Department of NUI Maynooth in co-operation with fifteen post-primary schools in three regions of Leinster. Its active phase concluded in Summer 2007. An interim report on the project's work, *Voices from School*, was published in September 2005, to share with colleagues in Ireland and farther afield the more salient issues the project encountered in its first two years. *Voices from School* focused on the insights gained in these years from a range of pioneering initiatives with the participating teachers and school leaders. These insights in turn furnished some important lessons for enhancing educational practice, and for educational planning and policy-making. Two further years of work have now served to deepen and refine the emergent lessons of the project's early stages. They have also yielded more insights in the form of new evidence from innovative educational practices in Irish school settings.

A feature of the project's work from the outset has been a commitment to regular consultation with national educational bodies, including the Inspectorate of the Department of Education and Science, the National Council for Curriculum and Assessment, the National Association of Principals and Deputy Principals, the managerial bodies, the teacher unions, national support agencies such as the School Development Planning Initiative, Leadership Development for Schools and the Second Level Support Service. In keeping with that consultative approach, this final report, compiled by seven members of the project team, seeks to present not only the yield of evidence gathered over four years of developmental work with teachers and school leaders. It also seeks to capture the fruits of our continuing discussions of this emergent yield with the main educational agencies in Ireland, as well as with the project's National Advisory Committee and International Consultative Panel.

It is necessary to say a word here about the project's workshop structure, as a basic familiarity with this is needed to understand many of the details presented in the following chapters. The project began its active phase in late 2003 by enlisting ten participant teachers, in five pairs, from each of 15 schools. In each case the pairings were: Principal and Deputy Principal, two teachers of maths, two teachers of science, two teachers of Irish, two teachers of English. Regular out-of-school workshops in these five areas enabled teachers to engage with colleagues from other schools in an ongoing way on issues of teaching and learning, and such sessions remained a feature of the project until its conclusion. The ICT strand of the project, which commenced in September 2005, enabled teachers from additional subject areas to enlist as participants and to become more active in advancing new initiatives within their schools. The workshops for participants in the ICT strand were school-based, and took account of the facilities available in particular schools. As the project progressed efforts were made to widen developmental initiatives to include the whole school. Whole-school seminars were organised in individual schools for this purpose during the later stages of the project. These drew mainly on recent innovative work by staff members who were participants in the TL21 project, but also on work by staff members who were not, or whose association with the project was on a more informal basis.

The title of the report, *Learning Anew*, calls attention both to a subtle insight and to one of the more intractable obstacles that has to be tackled before genuine professional development work can find fertile ground. Taking the obstacle first, this is the notion that because one is already equipped with one's professional qualification and with many years of professional experience, there is really nothing new that one needs to learn, apart perhaps from some upskilling here and there. That obstacle was by no means a universal one for the TL21 project. But it was encountered quite frequently in our initial contacts with schools. Secondly, the insight, as the story recollected on the back cover suggests, is that being a teacher means being at heart a committed learner for all of one's career. The responsibility for cultivating this commitment and sustaining its productive exercise has to be shared, and in meaningful ways: between the individual practitioner and the agencies needed to support creative practices of teaching and learning. An important practical step in furthering both an

2

awareness and an ownership of such responsibility is distinguishing sufficiently clearly between the different kinds of need in continuing professional development, and then providing appropriately for each. On a basic analysis, as has been increasingly acknowledged in recent years, the different needs include at least the following three: the needs of the educational system nationally, the needs of the school as a learning community, the needs of the individual teacher. We hope the contents of this report illuminate some promising ideas for action in all three of these areas, where Irish post-primary education is concerned.

Chapter 1

The Project's Main Aims in Context

The TL21 project has sought chiefly to develop and sustain new practices for enhancing the quality of teaching and learning in Irish post-primary education. To avoid ambiguity it should be stressed from the start that this question of *quality* is different from that of the *effectiveness* of teaching and learning. In recent years Ireland's educational system has generally been more praised than criticised where effectiveness (measurable outcomes) is concerned, though there are some growing concerns recently about performance in some subjects, most notably mathematics. Where the experienced quality of learning is concerned however, post-primary teachers themselves widely acknowledge that all is not well in our schools. There are frequently voiced apprehensions by teachers about being forced to adopt practices dictated by examination pressures, as distinct from practices that are inherently educational. An indication of this malaise is provided by the OECD *Education at a Glance* report for 2003, the most recent issue of this annual publication to survey students' perceptions of the quality of teaching and learning. This disclosed that over two-thirds of Irish 15 year olds 'often feel bored' at school, while the OECD average for this was under 50% (OECD 2003, Table D5.4). How the issue of quality is related to that of effectiveness is a complex issue of course, about which we will have much to investigate in this report.

Following extensive discussions on planning in 2003, the TL21 project team refined the project's aims to two main ones: (a) to strengthen teachers' capacities as the authors of their own work; (b) to encourage students to become more active and responsible participants in their own learning. During the last two years of the project however, and particularly in the light of our ongoing discussions with diverse colleagues at home and abroad, we became convinced of the necessity to advance a third priority, wider in scope than the other two, namely the development and promotion of innovative teachers as a strategic national resource for what is now commonly called a 'learning society'. In this opening chapter it's worth exploring the significance of each of these aims. This will help to place the subsequent chapters in a richer context, and in particular the key suggestions for practice and policy arising from our four years of active work with the schools.

(a) Strengthening teachers' capacities as the authors of their own work

An aim such as this presupposes that teachers are currently not the authors of their own work to the extent that they might be; that the conduct of their work is too frequently determined by forces beyond the control of teachers themselves. This less than happy situation is masked somewhat by the prominence of phrases like the 'professional autonomy' of the teacher in the formal discourse of education. But the reality in schools habitually falls short of a professional autonomy that would clearly cast teachers as the authors of their own practice. The following four examples, each of which identifies a family of issues to be tackled by the project's initiatives, serve to illustrate the practical significance of the first of the project's aims.

Firstly, inherited practices of teaching and learning in Irish second-level schools have regularly tended to sideline imagination and originality and to make teachers functionaries of predictable, lacklustre routines. Again it should be stressed that this affects the quality, more so than the effectiveness of teaching and learning. And although a highly centralised curriculum and examination system imposes obvious constraints on teachers' discretion, comparative reports by the OECD suggest that this discretion is greater in Ireland than in many of the other OECD countries. Secondly, teachers in second-level schools have very largely been insulated and isolated from their professional colleagues. Their relationships with each other and with the principal and school authorities are often informal, indeed are more often than not on first-name terms. But these relationships have seldom been characterised by systematic collaboration on learning issues, or by self-evaluation and peer review, or by active involvement in school planning. Thirdly, modern communications technologies have been perceived as of marginal relevance, or even as an intrusion, by many teachers, as distinct from being availed of in normal practice as opportunities to add imagination, colour and energy to the quality of learning. Comparisons drawn in 2003 by the OECD for 15 year olds in 30 countries reveal that Ireland had the highest proportion of students (49%) who make 'rare or no use' of computers in school. (OECD, 2006, Table D.5.3). Fourthly, and not least, the exercise of school leadership is commonly beset by an institutionalised rift between work that is essentially administrative in character and action that is essentially educational in character. Significantly, the increase in administrative work resulting from the education legislation of recent years has tended further to bureaucratise the job of Principal, and just at the time when educational research internationally is accomplishing a striking consensus on the distinctive human qualities called for in the educational leaders of the future (e.g. Duignan 2007; Fullan 2003; Lieberman & Miller 2004; Stoll, Fink & Earl, 2003).

So the first of the project's aims is concerned with the advancement of practices that are both emancipatory and developmental. As we shall explain in the course of this report, such advancements are not of the kind that can be accomplished once-and-for-all, but rather remain ever vulnerable to relapse; for instance where the predominant ethos is one of handling administrative demands (as in many school leaderships), or one of extrinsic pressures for performances in tests and examinations (as in most environments of post-primary teaching, and not just in examination classes). For this reason we shall be giving a particular importance to the question of sustainability and further development of the kinds of pedagogical and leadership practices promoted during the project's work.

(b) Encouraging students as active and responsible participants in learning

We have referred in the Introduction to the high degree of boredom among Irish fifteen-year old students reported by the OECD. Apart from courses like the Transition Year and the Leaving Certificate Applied, Irish post-primary students are infrequently active participants in the learning they carry out in school. That is not to say that the students don't work. Some work very hard indeed but often bypass the real and enduring benefits of their studies as they become habituated in a national preoccupation with extrinsic rewards and prizes. Inspectors' reports on different subjects in recent years have called attention to a predominance of passive learning on the part of students. In the last two years, with a fall in the numbers applying for places in higher education, the national news media have emphasised 'the end of the points race as we know it', and have conveyed the message that the points system now holds something for almost every student. What remains largely unremarked however is the question of how well or ill-equipped school leavers are to benefit from what third third-level education – with its intrinsic demands for self-sustaining learning – has to offer. Although the high non-completion of the 1990s have declined considerably (Morgan et al. 2001; OECD 2007), it is noteworthy that traditional styles of teaching and learning are prevalent at third level (IUA, 2005). Concerns have been increasingly voiced moreover that standards in undergraduate courses have been relaxed, enabling many students who would have in the past received pass grades in their final examinations to graduate with honours (Ireland.com 'Head2Head' website, archive for 23/4/07). Though this point remains controversial, what is beyond doubt is that the capacity to engage in autonomous learning enables one both to identify high standards and to apply them productively in one's own work

The deeper, or longer term significance of involving students as active and responsible participants in their own learning goes beyond these matters however. It concerns the cultivating of an abiding disposition that has at least two critical aspects. In the first place, developing a capacity for self-directed learning provides one with invaluable resources not merely for making informed choices in life and work, but also for recognising and nurturing what is most promising in one's own humanity. Secondly, such a capacity has as much, if not more importance in one's life as an adult than in one's years in formal education; all the more so in a society that can undergo in a decade or so the kinds of changes that would previously have been those of a generation. If the years of formal education neglect the cultivation of this disposition, notwith-standing how impressive they might be in terms of effectiveness,

7

the students are being sold short where the heart of the matter is concerned.

(c) Developing innovative teachers as a strategic national resource

In much of the official literature on 'the learning society' prominence is given to goals of economic and social policy (e.g. upskilling of vocational expertise, combating social exclusion through new access to training, treating investment in training like investment in capital). In this way formal education frequently comes to be viewed as part of the machinery for advancing these goals. This kind of macro perspective however, despite its currency in international policy discourse and official initiatives, remains foreign to the concerns of most teachers. Teachers focus primarily on the students they have to teach: on particulars like names, faces, individual and group characteristics. Within this micro context moreover, as the TL21 project's efforts in promoting innovative pedagogies brought home to us, post-primary teachers' practical priorities are especially responsive to what the assessment system is perceived to reward.

Our growing awareness that the workplace cultures of teachers and those of policy-making and implementation are largely unacquainted with each other, and are sometimes even worlds apart, alerted us to the necessity to elucidate a third aim for the project. As the teachers engaged in participatory professional development on a regular basis, it was notable that the insularity of their professional lives – often a self-protective one – yielded progressively to a desire for recurrent co-operation and regular networking with colleagues. With this broadening of perspective came a new awareness among many of the project's participants, including the project team, of the imaginative power of learning environments that were characterised by an ongoing commitment to collaboration and innovation. The project team noticed in such learning environments a special kind of potential and this became a focus for attention in the team's later debates and consultations.

In the latter half of the project there were two formal rounds of consultations with the national educational agencies and the International Consultative Panel (Autumn-Winter of 2005 and of 2006). In addition there were the scheduled meetings of the project's National Advisory Committee and many informal contacts with staff in the national agencies. These consultations brought home to us that the potential of such active learning environments was not merely local – i.e. confined to the individual schools. The heart of this fresh realisation can be summarised as follows: a teaching force where imaginative energies are continually renewed constitutes a strategic national resource of first importance. It is difficult to identify comparable resources in today's post-industrial societies, so perhaps the most telling comparison to draw is with what a country's reserves of mineral wealth represented in an industrial age. A major difference however is that teachers constitute a 'renewable' resource – though essentially to the extent to which the necessary resources and organised energies are committed to such renewal.

In articulating this third aim, we are conscious that it differs in at least one key respect from the other two, namely that it is a task of national scope. It will hopefully be clear to readers in the following chapters that the project's achievements under the first two aims provide a fund of promising possibilities for action, based on recent experience in Irish school settings. The proper achievement of the third aim however, lies beyond the capacity of the project's leaders and participants. It identifies a central as distinct from a subsidiary place for education in Ireland's current *National Development Plan 2007-2013.* This is to make a case, on strategic national grounds as well as on educational grounds, for a continuing professional development system for Ireland's teaching force that is among the best of its kind internationally. Reading the 2005 OECD report, *Teachers Matter: Attracting, Developing and Retaining Effective Teachers,* reminds one that Ireland is still favourably advantaged in the quality of its teachers. Ireland, it would seem, has not only a what economists call a 'comparative advantage' in its teachers, but possibly an 'absolute advantage'. Either way, in an age of globalisation, making the most of such an advantage should feature much more prominently than it does in the country's national development priorities.

Projects such as *Teaching and Learning for the 21ˢᵗ Century* are essentially temporary arrivals on the educational scene. Their real significance lies not in their immediate impact, which is necessarily small-scale, but in their legacies. The success of the TL21 project can ultimately be judged therefore by the extent to which the kinds of ongoing practices it successfully nurtured among small groups of teachers and school leaders become a defining feature of Ireland's provision for 21st century continuing professional development for teachers.

Chapter 2

Developing Educational Leadership at School Level

(1) Overview of main developments

In addition to regular workshops carried out with the participating teachers, the TL21 project included a series of afternoon seminars for school Principals and Deputy Principals – 3 per year – on the leadership of learning. There were also dedicated sessions for Principals and Deputy Principals, featuring leading international and national figures, at the project's overnight seminars in Maynooth each September and May. In the beginning the afternoon leadership seminars were held as plenary sessions in Maynooth and concentrated on the question of applying to Irish post primary schools the chief findings of recent international research on educational leadership. As the project progressed however it was found more fruitful to hold these seminars as smaller sessions on a regional basis: Midlands, Maynooth and Dublin. The continuity between one seminar and the next enabled a trusting rapport to become a feature of the seminars. This encouraged a frank sharing of experiences ('warts and all' as one Principal put it) between the school leaders on the progress of new initiatives in their schools. At the conclusion of the project's active phase (Summer 2007) many Principals and Deputies spoke of their own accord of the value of the regional seminars and expressed the wish to continue such networks into the future.

Amongst the most prominent of the project's early findings was the unsurprising one that the extent of its influence in the schools was directly linked to the quality and amount of the energies put into its various initiatives by the school leaderships. Related to this was the realisation that Principals and Deputies were in the best position to provide ongoing assessments of the wider changes in practice brought about these initiatives. At the mid-point of the project the evidence we gathered from school leaders spoke encouragingly of the project's benefits, particularly the progress in tackling the insulation and isolation of teachers. The recurrent and intensifying nature of the project's activities were critical here. This evidence also highlighted some constraints and obstacles faced by school leaders; not least the difficulty of finding time for professional development activities in an already crowded school calendar (See 'Responses from Principals and Deputy Principals' in the closing pages, pp.53-62 of *Voices from School* at www.nuim.ie/TL21).

In September 2007, following the completion of the project's scheduled work with the schools, Principals and Deputies were again surveyed for an overview of its main effects. A five-point questionnaire was designed, based on the project's main aims, and this was sent to each Principal and Deputy Principal in the fifteen schools in September 2007. It is acknowledged that on some issues in the survey, it is difficult for school leaders to give an estimate that is both comprehensive and accurate. Yet, allowing for this, it is important to have, at the end of the project, an estimation of its effects by the leaders of the participating schools.

Respondents could reply to the survey anonymously if they wished, but were asked to say whether the response was completed by Principal, or Deputy Principal, or both. Over half chose to identify themselves in their responses, either with a covering note or by signing the survey itself. Respondents were also invited to add any additional comments they wished, and about half chose to do so. Apart from those who had already submitted responses and had identified themselves in so doing, all the other schools were contacted in October and were asked to return completed questionnaires if they had not already done so.

Ten responses were received from Principals, and three of these were joint responses on behalf of Principal and Deputy Principal. In order to compare like with like in our calculating of the responses, each joint response was considered as two identical responses. Six responses were received from Deputy Principals, including two which were joint responses on behalf of Deputy Principal and Principal. The same principle for calculating was applied here. This makes a response rate of twenty-two out of a possible total of thirty. It may be that some of the other responses received from individual Principals or Deputy Principals were intended as joint responses, but if this was not stated, they were treated as single responses. It is quite possible that all schools were represented in the responses. It is difficult to say with certainty, as some respondents chose to exercise the option of anonymity. Our best judgement is that at least one response was received from either all schools or from fourteen of the fifteen.

Survey of Principals and Deputy Principals on the main effects of the TL21 Project, September/October 2007

The main effects of the TI21 project in our school can be seen in:

	Major	Significant	Minor
Active and regular work by subject teams on teaching and learning issues (22 responses) :	13	9	0
Sharing of ideas and practices with colleagues outside of one's own subject (22 responses) :	5	10	7
Improvements in students' attitudes and practices in learning (22 responses) :	6	10	6
Improvements in students' achievements in learning (21 responses):	4	10	7
To what extent has involvement in the project influenced your understanding of your role as an educational leader: (22 resp.)	16	6	0

Taking these five headings in turn, the findings on the first show that the biggest gains have been in promoting regular collaboration among teachers through working in subject teams on teaching and learning issues. The best results here were achieved where school leaders took early initiatives to bring about such collaboration and then continued to support its growth. There has been encouraging progress also on the issue of sharing ideas and practices with colleagues outside of one's own subject area. This is a more ambitious goal than sharing within subject teams, because in addition to the cultivation among teachers of a disposition to share more widely, it also calls for more extensive preparatory work by school leaderships. For instance it requires carefully-planned whole-school seminars, as distinct from subject team meetings, to provide meaningful opportunities for such wider sharing. The 'rotation seminars' organised in a number of the schools in the later stages of the project – described in section (2) of this chapter and in Appendix A at the end – proved to be a particularly useful strategy for this purpose.

Impressive progress was made also in most of the schools in bringing about improvements in students' attitudes and practices in learning, though differences between schools, and between subjects, are evident in this. On the whole however, where teachers persevered with innovative pedagogical approaches there were salutary changes in students' attitudes and practices and notable improvements in the learning environments where the new approaches became a growing feature of daily life. Again, active encouragement by school leaderships, together with ongoing constructive feedback at workshops, were critical factors here. Where the achievements of students are concerned, progress is more difficult to assess on a whole-school basis. But the responses from school leaders have clearly identified instances of significant improvements in students' achievements that can be attributed to the sustained adoption of new approaches by particular teachers, especially some specific approaches from the assessment for learning family (AfL) during the last two years of the project. (Changes in students' learning practices and achievements are reviewed in detail in Chapter 4.)

Finally, the question to school leaders on how much their involvement in the project influenced their own understanding of their leadership role yielded revealing insights. All respondents reported positively on this, with sixteen describing the change in their understanding of their role as major, and six as significant. Many of the comments offered by the school leaders are either paraphrased or quoted in the following sections of this chapter.

(2) Developing leadership capacity and promoting leadership initiatives in schools

We mentioned in passing in the previous chapter that the international literature on educational leadership in recent years has produced a striking consensus in its findings. Two notable features of this consensus are: (i) the necessity for leadership to focus purposefully and incisively on quality-of-learning issues (as distinct for instance from aligning leadership practices to externally- mandated directives); (ii) the range of distinctive human qualities called for in today's educational leaders. These latter include things like: an imaginative and robust educational vision; deep reserves of moral courage and energy; a trusting disposition capable of nurturing active co-operation and leadership capability among others; a commitment to building and sustaining high-quality learning environments; a proficiency in strategic thinking and planning; a discerning responsiveness to a wide variety of expectations and demands; a highly-developed capacity for con-structive criticism, including perceptive self-criticism (Duignan 2007; Fullan 2003; Lieberman & Miller 2004; MacBeath 2006; Starratt 2004; Stoll, Fink & Earl, 2003).

Qualities such as these are best cultivated in learning environments that already exhibit some of them, at least in some degree. Where qualities of a contrary kind are to the fore however, whether through bureaucracies in management practice or through extrinsic pressures, the climate is less hospitable to promoting high quality educational leadership. Though other countries might fare considerably worse than Ireland in this regard, the ubiquity of administrative demands that attends the work of Irish school leaders creates particular difficulties, both for taking leadership initiatives and for developing leadership capacity. Initiatives thus have to be devised to create new conditions, or more subtly, to enable new conditions to find fertile root. This issue is considered in more detail in section (3) of the present chapter, but it is important to mention it initially here to fill in a key detail of the context in which the leadership activities of the TL21 project were carried out. In this present section then, we will focus firstly (a) on the development of leadership capacity with Principals and Deputy Principals and secondly (b) on the promotion of leadership initiatives within the schools.

(2 a) *The development of capacity through leadership seminars:*
The project's work began in November 2003, with the first of the seminars for Principals and Deputy Principals. The experience of

earlier, smaller-scale projects which had concentrated on curricular and pedagogical initiatives (e.g. *School and Curriculum
Development* 1995-2001), made it clear that it was important to
include a school leadership dimension as an integral part of any
such future undertakings; not only that, but also that the school
leaders' participation would have to be *as leadership practitioners*,
rather than as facilitators who might then delegate the steering of
the project's work in the school to someone else.

In the first year of the project the leadership seminars brought
the Principals and Deputy Principals of the fifteen participating
schools together on three occasions for plenary sessions in
Maynooth. These were afternoon sessions of three-hours duration
and they concentrated firstly on reviewing the qualities stressed by
the international research on leadership. This was done with a
view to strengthening these qualities in the Principals' and Deputy
Principals' work with teacher colleagues in their own schools. The
practice of Principal and Deputy devoting an hour per week to
discussions with each other on teaching and learning initiatives in
the school was recommended from the start. The workshops for
teacher participants got under way early in 2004 and from this
point onwards the specific priorities for school leaders included
consulting regularly with the participating teachers from their
schools, encouraging them in taking new initiatives, and
monitoring the progress of these initiatives.

The plenary seminars in Maynooth for school leaders
included dedicated time for sharing experiences and perspectives,
and the participants at each seminar were divided into three
groups for this purpose, with a deliberate mix of participants from
the different regions in each group. It was felt that this would
encourage a more frank exchange between the school leaders, as
comparative issues that might constrain the quality of discussion
between schools in the same geographical area would now be less
of an issue. Experience proved otherwise. Towards the latter part
of Year 2 it became apparent that, whatever about the merits of
mixing school leaders from different regions, the leaders
themselves were now keen to meet on a regional basis, and to
share progress reports with their local counterparts on a recurring
basis. The third session of Year 2 was therefore organised as three
regional seminars and the success of these ensured that this

regional model was adopted for the remainder of the project. The later sessions for the school leaders witnessed fluent and well-focused exchanges on issues such as those included in the survey reported above, and were particularly rich as professional learning environments.

(2 b) *Leadership initiatives in the schools:*

By the half-way stage (Summer 2005) good progress was made in most schools on the issue of ongoing collaborative work in subject teams on quality-of-learning issues. These collaborations, it should be emphasised, included not just the school's participants in the TL21 workshops, but also their teaching colleagues within the school in the relevant subject. To advance the sharing of ideas and experiences *across* subject boundaries in a school was a more difficult task however. This aim was promoted through a major focus during the second two years on innovations drawing on generic teaching approaches, particularly those from the assessment for learning family (AfL), on which there has recently been much promising research internationally. As teachers began to incorporate such approaches more systematically into their practice (some had already been using many of them in an implicit way), school leaders considered ways in which the emergent benefits of these initiatives might best be shared with colleagues on a whole-school basis. Dedicated time at school staff meetings, with opportunities for individual teachers to report on their experiences, provided some readily available means to enable such sharing. These were not the most effective means however, as the opportunities for sustained engagement with specific issues are quite limited at such large assemblies.

In due course we devised the idea of 'rotation seminars', and these proved to be a much more effective way for progress on recent innovations by particular teachers to be shared with all colleagues in a school. This model provides for a few simultaneous workshops (45-50 mins.) to be run a few times on a rotation basis during a staff development day. Each workshop is hosted by a teacher, or pair of teachers, with some fresh ideas from their own recent practice to share with colleagues. The host teachers repeat the workshops so that each group of teachers can participate in each workshop in turn during the course of the day.

By May 2007, rotation seminars in one variation or another had been held in seven of the fifteen schools and were being actively considered for the 2007-08 year in three others. The following comment from a Principal on the consequences of such seminars is representative of many others: 'It was particularly effective, in that it allowed for a shift in perspective in relation to planning by departments rather than a series of individuals following their own plans. More importantly, this initiative can now be built upon at future staff days'. A practical example of how a staff development day might be planned and carried out as a series of rotation seminars is contained in Appendix 5 at the end of this report.

Before concluding this section of the chapter a few comments are called for on the significance of what we have just been considering. Firstly, activities such as rotation seminars represent an exercise in advanced collaborative planning among school leaders and teachers. They are in a very productive sense a form of learning-by-doing, both for school leaders and for the particular teachers who host the workshops. The prospect of hosting such a workshop can of course be a bit daunting for teachers. Our experience has shown however that the active assistance of school leaders in planning such sessions can turn this to advantage. This is achieved by emphasising the opportunities for the host teachers to take meaningful leadership initiatives that wouldn't otherwise arise; opportunities that develop these teachers' own capacities as educational leaders. Moreover, where an exercise such as a rotation seminar has proved a fruitful event in a school it helps to raise to a higher plane teachers' appreciation of the real meaning of continuing professional development. This is all the more so when such events are organised on a continuing basis, or better still, when they can be included at scheduled intervals in the school's yearly calendar.

Secondly, the success of initiatives like rotation seminars in the later stages of the project provided much stimulating material for exchange at the more recent of the regional seminars for Principals and Deputy Principals. Participants at these showed a natural willingness to contribute stories from their own schools and a healthy eagerness to ask about what factors made for success, what pitfalls had to be avoided and so on. In other words the increased energy that the leadership seminars had gained since becoming more informal regional events was further added to by an increasing supply of promising ideas and frank questions in the later seminars. A typical comment, this time from one of the joint responses, puts the point like this: 'We were heavily influenced by others in the network. It was heartening to know that we had issues in common, as well as identifying that we must be doing some things well'.

Finally, it is tempting to conclude that regular regional meetings of this kind for school leaders could continue as self-sustaining professional development networks. A desire for such continuity has been clearly voiced by many of the school leaders. But such sessions need to be planned and co-ordinated, either by one of the participants acting in turn as convenor, or more practically under the auspices of a national support agency; ideally perhaps through the co-operative auspices of the relevant agencies at regional or more local level. The experience of the TL21 project has shown that such sessions are particularly fruitful when they involve the leaders of five or so schools who have come to know each other informally, as well as knowing and respecting each other as professionals. Of course an existing group could be joined by a new school, or an existing group might in time divide and form the basis of two new groups. But it is important to keep the groups sufficiently small to allow meaningful involvement by each school during a normal session of a few hours. Considerations like these underline the desirability of constructive involvement, though not necessarily control, by the relevant support agencies.

(3) Tensions between demands of leadership and administration

In the project's interim report, *Voices from School* (2005), the tensions between the demands of leadership and those of administration were identified as an acute issue for school Principals and Deputy Principals. In addition to the evidence gathered through the project's own work on this issue, we cited reports such as Leader and Boldt (1992), McManamly/SLSS (2002) and the Joint Managerial Body (2005). This evidence underlined the point that the kinds of leadership efforts required to enhance the quality of teaching and learning in Ireland's post-primary schools were being seriously hindered by demands on school leaders to give their time and energies to something else – chiefly to administrative work. In the two further years since 2005, the administrative pressures on school leaders have increased rather than decreased, not least because of the accumulating practical consequences of new legislation such as the Education Welfare Act (2000) and the Education for Persons with Special Educational Needs Act (2004).

It is against this background that the school leaders involved in the TL21 project sought to promote a range of initiatives to enrich the learning environments in their schools, particularly those initiatives that advanced different forms of collaboration among teachers and productive changes in students' attitudes and learning practices. As shown in the first section of this chapter, these advances were major or significant in over two-thirds of the participating schools, with developments in some specific areas in the remaining schools. In the cases where the developments were minor, this was invariably associated with an inability on the part of school leaderships to engage 'hands on', or in a sustained way, with the initiatives the project was seeking to advance. In the cases where development were significant or major, school leaders had to engage in ongoing struggles to create the time and the opportunities for new initiatives to take wing and to become prominent in the school's professional culture. Such struggles included most notably battling continually with the press of administrative necessities and daily urgencies, or giving thought and energy to overcoming or circumventing various kinds of resistance among some members of school staff.

Certainly the leaders had to be supported in such struggles by the project team, but not in the form of hand-holding; rather through consultation, planning and feedback, through periodic visits to the schools for meetings with small or larger groups, and not least through providing workshops and seminars that were marked by continuity and active participation. In some instances it was possible to link this support work to developments that were already underway in schools with the assistance of the School Development Planning Initiative. Reviewing the manner in which the more successful leadership initiatives were carried out, the factors that emerge as the most important are: clarity of purpose in planning a particular intervention or initiative, constancy in the face of difficulties encountered and continuity of support to those engaged in it.

In the light the lessons learned over the four years of the project's work, it important to stress now that the conflict between the demands of leadership and those of administration is not just an issue for school Principals and Deputy Principals. In differing ways it is also an issue for other parties, including those affected by its consequences and those in a position to influence changes in the conditions under which schools carry out their work. The first group mainly comprises the teachers and students who are disadvantaged by an inability, or curtailed capacity, on the part of school leaderships to put the enhancement of quality in learning at the heart of the school's developmental goals and to keep it there. Secondly, and crucially, there are the policymakers and educational authorities (e.g. DES, VECs, SEC), whose decisions and regulations influence directly the conditions in which educational leadership can be exercised – fruitfully or frustratingly as the conditions themselves permit.

Finally, the degree of attention which it was possible for the TL21 team to give to the participating schools would not be possible to replicate on a nationwide basis through the support agencies. Nor would it be appropriate to do so. The TL21 project was a *research*, as well as a development project. Because of this, and of the relatively short time-scale of the project, it was necessary to undertake a number of initiatives in the schools at the same time and to track these closely to gather practical research evidence from Irish circumstances. Leadership interventions can be designed on a smaller or larger scale and their sequencing can be adapted to local circumstances and possibilities. The critical points are: (a) that the preparatory thinking-through and assembled energies are well-matched to the scope of the initiative being undertaken; and (b) that there is some reliable provision for monitoring and for periodic support. Both requirements call for the involvement not so much of a university research team (though that can have added advantages), but of a relevant educational support agency which has sufficient resources to meet just such requirements. None of this takes from the necessity for measures at a national level to relieve the burden of administration on school leaders. Simply put, the locales where school Principals and Deputy Principals work have to be rendered more hospitable to their primary purpose, namely the exercise of innovative educational leadership.

(4) Issues of time and planning

It is instructive to recall that at the commencement of the TL21 project, schools did not, for the most part, rush to become participants. In order to secure the participation of fifteen schools, approaches had to be made over a period of time to almost double that number. In no case did any of the school leaders who were approached think the project was a misconceived under-taking. Those who declined to participate invariably did so with reluctance, the most common reasons being that the time couldn't be found, that the project would be an 'add-on' to an already tightly-packed school schedule. A critical response to this might be that school leaders had become so immersed in a world of administration that they could not discern the thrust of the project's work, or see how it might help make their own work less rather than more burdensome. And that seems to be largely true in the case of some of the school Principals who declined to become participants. At the same time, signing up for this project did mean some extra time commitments for school leaders and for participating teachers. Following a round of planning discussions with the managerial bodies and teacher unions in 2003, the schedule of workshops and seminars we designed sought to cause minimum disruption to a school year that was 'already heavily eroded with in-service work', as one of the bodies put it. Consequently, a combination of in-school time and out-of-school time was decided on for the workshops. This combination was kept under review, and further adjustments were made at two points during the project's lifetime.

There was an average attendance of 73% at workshops for teachers and an average of 71% at seminars for school leaders over the duration of the project. In the case of non-attendance by a Principal or Deputy the chief reason was the occurrence of something in the school that required one or both to remain on the school premises. In the case of teachers, absences were attributable mainly to: (a) family commitments (for workshops in out-of-school time); (b) temporary staff shortages in school (precluding release for workshops held during part of the school day); (c) a temporary or longer-term drop in personal motivation (for both kinds of workshops). Despite the difficulties associated with scheduling workshops and seminars at times when participants were free to attend, the workshops and the seminars proved to be a very successful feature of the project.

Another difficulty under the time and planning heading was finding time within the school week for developmental things like critical friend meetings, or small group meetings to review tasks-in-progress and plan new initiatives, or the writing up of summary reports on progress. As distinct from workshops and seminars where new forms of professional development are studied and analysed, these school-based exercises are cases of professional development in action, but as a part of the normal school day or week. Current conditions of employment state that the maximum time for scheduled teaching by post-primary teachers is 22 hours per week. It is clearly that case however that teachers' actual working week greatly exceeds this, and in many cases exceeds the European average of 38½ hours. Because of the prominence of the 22 hours issue however, to suggest that some time should be scheduled to provide opportunities for planning and review activities by teachers can be seen by many as a suggestion for an 'add-on' to an already full weekly schedule. Yet the fact remains that a programme of continuing professional development that involves workshops for the study and analysis of innovative practices will necessarily involve *some* time commitment from practitioners; time that is distinct from that which is already taken up by the school timetable.

Drawing on various kinds of ingenuity school leaders in the TL21 project were able find ways to release teachers to engage in professional development workshops off-campus, or in meetings within the school, during the normal school day. And sometimes they were just unable to find this room for manoeuvre. Notwithstanding the fruits of such ingenuity, the fact remains that 'release' of this kind is a taking-away of teachers from work they are already scheduled for, and it invariably means a loss of teaching time to students. This an issue of national scope, and it is taken up again in chapters 5 and 7. At this point we would just note that the concept of 'release' for teachers, for all its prominence in the vocabulary of in-service education, tends to obscure the real potential of continuing professional development itself.

By way of conclusion, if teachers' professional time in the 21st century is to be distributed between time for teaching and for a range of professional activities with colleagues – including out-of-school workshops and in-school developmental activities – then a clear acknowledgement of this has to become part of the professional mentality of teaching itself. This shift of thinking means that provision for such a range of professional development activities has to be made in the school timetable and the yearly school calendar, as is already the case in best international practice. Such a shift also has wide implications for the teaching profession as a whole, including for such things as conditions of service, remuneration, career structure and promotion, accreditation for professional development achievements. An inescapable consequence is the necessity to re-conceive and re-negotiate at least some of teachers' conditions of employment for the 21st century, to reflect the varied nature of teachers' professional work at present and for the future.

(5) Leadership training and renewal: the importance of co-operation

We have already suggested that leadership capacities are best nurtured in environments where there is already something of an ethos of innovation, or where the work climate is hospitable to fresh initiatives. We have also seen that where conditions don't favour such initiatives – whether because of bureaucratic practices or of escalating administrative pressures – steps have to be taken, adroitly but decisively, to create the conditions. Being capable of taking such steps and of sustaining new developments that have been got under way distinguishes a capacity for leadership from the more everyday attributes of management and administration.

As with most forms of human accomplishment, unless innovative educational leadership is regularly practised, the capacities nurtured by such practice will wane. This is not to say that school leaders thus become indolent. Rather it is to point out that the bulk of their time becomes absorbed in practising expertise of a more routine kind; not because of a desire to do so but because of a perceived necessity to do so in order to keep trouble at bay. In this way strong *cultures* of administration frequently grow where vibrant cultures of educational leadership need to flourish.

This discloses a threefold necessity in leadership development in education. Firstly there is the necessity to develop a leadership-of-learning capacity – among Principals, Deputy Principals, aspirant leaders, middle leaders – through training workshops that focus on the study and analysis of leadership ideas and leadership practice. Secondly there is the necessity to strengthen leadership-in-action in specific school settings. Thirdly there is the necessity to promote local networks (informal or more formal) for the regular renewal of leadership capability. These would involve an exchange of practical leadership achievements among experienced leaders who are actively involved in innovation, or are becoming so. The first kind of necessity was the focus of the early seminars for school leaders in the TL21 project. The second kind of necessity increasingly became the focus of these seminars as the seminars themselves came more and more to resemble informal networks during the final stages of the project. This latter development, in turn, points to the merits of local networks for school leaders.

Active pursuit of the first necessity is now evident in much of the work of the support agency Leadership Development for Schools (LDS), which has grown steadily in recent years and continues to expand and diversify. Work on the second necessity, the strengthening of leadership capacity in practical ways in schools, is being advanced by the work of the School Development Planning Initiative, and also by recommendations from the Inspectorate after Whole School Evaluations and subject inspections. All three agencies remain keenly in touch with research perspectives on educational leadership, and all three have continually taken an active interest in the emergent findings of the TL21 project. This kind of unforced co-operation was a feature of our work over the last four years that we warmly recall.

The TL21 project concludes at a time of transition in post-primary education in Ireland. Mindful of the temporary nature of the project's involvements, we are happy to have had some role to play in that transition. We have good reason to believe that the kind of professional co-operation that grew between ourselves and the support agencies, and between the agencies themselves, can be encouraged to new levels in the future and with very positive consequences for the quality of teaching and learning in schools. We have some suggestions to make on this in the final chapter.

Chapter 3

Promoting New Practices among Teachers

(1) Overview of main developments

The interim report of September 2005, *Voices from School*, recorded that encouraging progress was made in the first two years of the project on tackling two important issues of customary practice. These were the insulation and isolation of teachers from colleagues and the conformist tenor of much teaching and learning in post-primary schools. That report provided individual accounts by different members of the project team on advances made in the teaching of English, Irish, Maths and Science. It also gave an account of progress in the project's ICT strand, which got under way a half-year after workshops commenced in the original four subjects. Among the advances highlighted, and documented with retrospective comments from teachers themselves, were: working in subject teams or subject departments, as distinct from planning and reviewing in isolation; critically reviewing one's own practice, sometimes with a 'critical friend'; gradually introducing new initiatives in one's teaching and monitoring the effects of these on learners and on the learning environment in the class; sharing the findings of such monitoring with teachers from other schools at the project's workshops; trying out in one's own practice ideas that other teachers have reported favourably on at workshops; using feedback from students – both senior cycle and junior cycle – in developing and refining new pedagogical approaches. For any readers not familiar with the term 'critical friend' the following definition, taken from the research literature, may be helpful: 'a trusted person who asks provocative questions, provides data to be examined through another lens, and offers critique of a person's work as a friend'. (Costa & Kallick, 1993, p.50)

In the second half of the project's life, its work with participating teachers has been marked firstly by attempts to develop to advanced levels practices such as those just outlined. Secondly, there has been a drive since September 2005 to shift the emphasis from the teaching of individual subjects to pedagogical issues more generically. While workshops in the four original subjects have remained a feature of the project, the emphasis in these workshops has moved to teaching approaches that can be used in a range of different subjects. In particular, participating teachers have been encouraged to share progress reports on their initiatives with colleagues from different subject areas in their own schools. The rotation seminars referred to in the previous chapter have proved to be a productive way of accomplishing this, especially where such seminars are strongly promoted by the school leadership.   The ICT strand of the project has also shifted emphasis during the second half of the project. While the *Digital Resource* initiative of the earlier stages enabled teachers to conduct selective web searches and incorporate the fruits of these into their own teaching approaches, the later *Linking4Learning* initiative was designed to encourage teachers and students to work collaboratively to create their own web pages. This allowed teachers from a range of different subjects to participate in specific practical explorations, especially ones that sought to discover fresh learning possibilities in areas of the syllabus that may have come to be seen as rather lustreless.

Under the headings outlined below, this chapter will review both the developments that took place in teaching approaches among the project's participants and the measures adopted to bring about and sustain such developments.

(2) Using a workshop model to stimulate new pedagogical initiatives

From the preparatory work done in advance of the project, it was clear that if the taking-on of new initiatives were to succeed in meaningful ways, means would have to be found for dismantling inherited attitudes that secluded teachers' daily professional practices from each other, and that militated against innovation. The first workshops therefore concentrated largely on obtaining informal accounts from teachers on apparently mundane (i.e. unthreatening) matters, like the kinds of textbooks and other resources they were using.   While these comparative accounts from the workshop participants confirmed that textbooks frequently took much of the real initiative in teaching away from teachers themselves, they also yielded a number of common concerns on which an agenda for active participation by teachers could be constructed. Such concerns included: questioning and its possible uses; sharing the burden of work (i.e. getting students to take more of it); availing of teaching colleagues for support and constructive criticism; finding new sources for practical ideas for teaching. By involving teachers from the start in constructing the agenda for the workshops the danger of a lecture-style format coming to dominate was avoided. This also laid foundations for a particular kind of learning climate, or ethos in the workshops; one that most participants contributed to building and sustaining, and indeed looked forward to returning to at scheduled intervals. Another benefit was that this approach got at prominent concerns like student discipline, not by confronting them directly, but by the backdoor as it were. In other words, by concentrating on constructive initiatives in *teaching* and *learning* that might be introduced gradually over a number of weeks, teachers found that discipline problems that were caused mainly by lack of motivation featured less and less in their work.

This point about introducing new developments in a gradual way is crucial. Discussions at the workshops helped to allay teachers' apprehensions that innovations had to be taken on all-at-once if they were to make an impact. Things were found to work best where a teacher might select an individual class (usually not an examination class) to try out a new approach, say with questioning, or group work, or using learning criteria, and where the approach might be monitored between one workshop and the next. Workshops thus became occasions not just for sharing progress reports on one's own work, but also occasions for gathering valuable ideas on initiatives tried by some of the other teachers in their own schools: on what might be promising things to try and on what pitfalls might be avoided. As the workshops progressed, teachers' capacities to introduce and develop creative innovations developed, slowly at first, but more significantly during the second and subsequent years of the project. In addition to developing a strong community spirit among participants, the continuity of relationships nourished by the workshops also meant that there were recurring informal contacts between many participants in the intervals between scheduled workshops. These contacts included widespread use of phone calls, text messaging, e-mails and, in the project's final year, the use of the Moodle electronic learning environment by some of the workshop groups.

Some difficulties to the continuity of workshops were caused by the departure of individual participants from one year to the next – through moving to other posts, changes in family circumstances and so on – and by the departure of one full-time member of the TL21 project team during the second year of the project. One of the lessons to be learned from this is that, while a suite of workshops designed to run with a given group of participants over the duration of a few school years can bring very significant benefits, there is also a need for shorter flexible, or modular structures in formal professional development programmes. Such flexibility would allow for any particular suite of workshops to start and finish with the school year itself. This would be attractive to greater numbers of teachers than would a two-year or three-year timescale, though appropriate adjustments would need to be made in the aims the suite of workshop was seeking to accomplish. Similarly, if an accreditation option were to be linked to a shorter series of workshops, the accreditation requirements would need to be proportionally adjusted.

(3) Cultivating constructive self-criticism

There is an abundant literature on 'reflective practice' in educational research, springing partly form Donald Schon's seminal study of 1984, *The Reflective Practitioner*, but also from a tradition of action research and self-evaluation in education that has grown steadily from the nineteen seventies onwards (Elliott, 1991). The recent nature of the terms 'action research' and 'reflective practitioner' suggest to many that what they involve are practices of modern origin, or even something temporarily fashionable. As the story recalled on the back cover of this report suggests however, the discipline of critical evaluation of one's actions as an educator with fellow learners is more ancient, and holds an importance and promise that have largely been eclipsed in the history of Western education. Such recollections remind us that getting this kind of discipline underway among practitioners, whether they are teachers, accountants, administrators, or whatever, is essentially about something more than technique, something beyond skills and competencies. In the last few years similar reminders were furnished regularly by the experience of the project's participants in their engagements with its two main aims.

Coming to see one's own work as a teacher through the eyes of others, including colleagues, students and indeed parents, certainly involves skill, even advanced skill. More importantly, it also involves what Plato memorably called 'turning around the eye of the soul' and enabling one's understanding to recognise things in fuller and deeper measure. Far from granting a superior intellectual certainty in which one can henceforth rest assured, such shifts in understanding begin to disclose a more challenging, yet a more beckoning kind of insight. This is the insight that probably what is most important in being a teacher is the necessity of remaining a learner for all of one's career. This involves not just keeping up with changes in the syllabus or with relevant developments in the subjects one is teaching. It also involves learning from one's colleagues and from one's students, among others, about the effects of one's own teaching, about short-comings as well as strengths in one's own practice, about the helpful as distinct from the hindering contributions students can make, about an abundance of ideas unthought of before in one's own mind.

The participatory nature of the project's workshops, and the informal contacts sustained by participants in the time between workshops, promoted environments conducive to this kind of learning. More formally, efforts were made to pair same-subject participants from individual schools as critical friends, and to designate one period during the week when both would be free to engage in scheduled critical friend meetings. This strategy worked well where the sessions were scheduled, though feedback from teachers, Principals and Deputy Principals revealed that such scheduling called for special adjustments to be made elsewhere in the timetable, and would be difficult to incorporate on a wide scale in school timetables. These difficulties were not so severe however as to preclude some variant of a critical friend approach as a specific requirement in those forms of professional development that would include an accreditation dimension. In many instances moreover, participation in scheduled critical friend meetings,

31

although discontinued in a second or later years of the project, had given teachers the capacity and the willingness to engage in such meetings on an informal basis when opportunities could be found.

It became clear in the project's later stages that while the capacity for self-evaluation and constructive criticism is fruitfully built through the continuity and rapport provided by small-scale workshop formats, advancing it on a whole-school basis requires action of another kind. In this connection it is important to develop procedures within the school that call for its exercise on a regular basis. Equally important are the informal networks that teachers themselves develop, whether or not arising out of their participation in formal continuing professional development initiatives. Each of these points has long-term implications for how the national support structures for continuing professional development are to be developed in the future.

(4) Building and sustaining subject departments and subject teams within schools

Prior to their involvement in the TL21 project, most of the participant teachers reported that their conversations in school on pedagogical issues were infrequent, unstructured, and rarely informed by ideas of active professional collaboration on teaching and learning issues. This is a common practical example of the insulation and isolation of teachers which the project sought to address. One of the more striking things to emerge during the first workshop sessions was that teachers found it much easier to talk about their work with same-subject colleagues from other schools than with similar colleagues within their own school. It emerged that while some schools had established subject departments, discussion at department meetings rarely focused on practices of teaching and learning. For the most part it focused on textbooks and resources, administration of tests and examinations, planning for coverage of the syllabus, and on other organisational matters.

As teachers began to take new initiatives with selected classes and to exchange progress reports and viewpoints on these on these at workshops, their readiness to engage in such conversations with colleagues within their own school also advanced. Increasingly, teachers at the workshops came to share perspectives not just on their own work but also on departmental initiatives on teaching and learning in their schools. In the leadership strand of the project, priority was also given at seminars for Principals and Deputy Principals to the development of subject teams in schools. In schools where these were already established and engaged with teaching and learning initiatives, the Principal and Deputy Principals were able to give reports on progress to date to their colleagues from other schools and to provide much practical advice in response to questions. The TL21 team organised seminars in a number of schools, following consultations with teachers and Principal in these schools, on the merits of subject teams and how they might best be developed. (Note: Sometimes there might be no difference in practice between a subject team and a subject department. At the same time, placing the emphasis on the team highlights proactive work over administrative structures, without however neglecting the latter). In workshop-type settings, these school-based seminars identified concrete ideas and suggestions for the promotion of subject teams in the schools. They also shared recent research findings on active learning with teachers and explored the importance of subject teams in the context of Whole School Evaluations and the recommendations on good practice contained in the *Report of the Chief Inspector 2001-2004* (DES, 2005, p.9).

As the survey of Principals and Deputy Principals cited at the beginning of Chapter 2 shows, successfully assisting schools in developing practices that sustain proactive subject teams was one of the major achievements of the TL21 project. While the practices promoted by the workshops were a key factor in this, equally important were the efforts of school Principals and Deputy Principals to find time on a recurring basis for meetings of subject teams. This involved much ingenuity, as in most cases some of the necessary time had to be taken from the existing school timetable, but in a way which would minimise the loss of teaching time to the students. There was widespread agreement among the project's participants that subject team meetings and associated planning and review activities should be regarded as important features of teachers' normal work, as distinct from optional 'add-ons'. The practical import of this is that such activities need to be scheduled into the normal school calendar, as now happens in standard practice in many other countries.

(5) Extending benefits of new practices to the whole school

We have mentioned above the initial reticence of teachers to share perspectives on their practices with same-subject colleagues. Such reticence was more pronounced when it came to sharing accounts of successful innovations in one's own practice with colleagues *outside* of one's own subject area. Most teachers had concerns that if they took the initiative on such wider sharing themselves they were likely to draw negative reactions: viewed by some of their colleagues as showing off, or as setting a standard that would show the work of colleagues in a poor light, or as attempting to advance their own careers at the expense of colleagues. It is revealing that while such concerns were not universal, they were sufficiently common as to constitute a serious obstacle. Again, they highlight the prevalence of professional insulation and isolation, as distinct from proactive professional co-operation, in the inherited cultures of post-primary education in Ireland.

It was clear that such obstacles needed to be tackled in a whole-school context, and to this end school leaders were encouraged, where necessary or appropriate, to prepare the ground for a specific kind of 'staff day': a seminar that would include members of the TL21 team in a support role, but that would have members of the school staff as the major contributors. The first of these seminars was organised on the rotation principle described in Chapter 1 above (section 2 b) and proved to be very successful. (See Appendix 5 for a summary of how a rotation seminar works in practice). Much of this success was due to the fact that the teachers who 'took the floor' to share their experiences with colleagues spoke frankly about their difficulties as well as their successes with new initiatives. Fears that colleagues might seize on any weaknesses turned out to be groundless, not least because of the constructive atmosphere established at the start of the seminar. Feedback from the school confirmed that the seminar proved to be very energising for the staff in general.

34

The success of this first rotation seminar provided additional impetus to efforts to get them underway in other schools, and by May 2007, rotation seminars in one variant or another had been held in seven of the fifteen participating schools and were being actively considered for the 2007-08 year in three others. The careful preparation required for such events cannot be over-emphasised, particularly the necessity to create a safe environment for a constructive exchange of ideas, for the raising of serious questions, and for the frank but productive voicing of any points of difference or disagreement. This is one of the reasons that the first of such seminars organised with the involvement of TL21 team members did not occur until early in the final year of the project's active life. As the later experience of the project shows, such seminars, if they take place at recurring intervals, can be a crucial means of long-term enhancement in the learning environments of schools, and of promoting a professional culture conducive to innovation.

Finally, it is likely that the professional capacities called for, both among teachers and school leaders, to engage in more advanced professional development activities of this kind, could be brought to a sufficient level of proficiency in a shorter timescale than what the TL21 project accomplished. A few brief historical points will help to illustrate this. A very different climate from today's prevailed in the Autumn of 2003. For instance, although the start of workshops for teachers was postponed from September 2003 to January 2004, many post-primary schools still showed serious scars of the then recent industrial dispute. Secondly, support agencies like Leadership Development for Schools and the School Development Planning Initiative, with whom the project developed many fruitful links, were still in their early days with small staffs, and had not yet had many opportunities to work with schools specifically on teaching and learning issues. Thirdly, Whole School Evaluations and subject inspections had not yet made the big impact they were due to make within the next few years. In each of these three respects the picture has changed significantly, though not entirely, since 2003 and there is now a more evident awareness among school communities about the desirability and the necessity for continuing professional development. In brief, conditions are more conducive now for initiatives that aim to build among teachers those professional capacities focused on whole-school development. To conclude, there are two key requirements for success in this undertaking. One is the necessity for scheduled time that allows for regularity and continuity of engagement by practitioners; a necessity that comes to the fore repeatedly in this report. The other is the provision of adequate and appropriate resources specifically for the second of the three main kinds of need in continuing professional development that we described in the Introduction, namely the needs of the school as a learning community.

(6) Advancing the use of ICT to enhance teaching and learning

Workshops in the ICT strand were organised on an individual school basis, and in each case after prior consultations with the schools. One of the points that had to be clarified at the start was that these workshops would concentrate not on basic computer skills, but on imaginative ways of drawing on ICT to provide a higher quality of learning for students. It wasn't always possible to maintain a clear distinction between these two however, as some additional basic skills had to be picked up by some participants during the course of workshops on new pedagogical approaches, as well as in the intervals between workshops. Though this could sometimes be a drawback, it often increased the amount of learning from one another at workshops. It was also necessary to emphasise in some cases that, while ICT could be used for a variety of administrative and record purposes by teachers, the emphasis in the TL21 project would be on its uses for teaching and learning.

Some schools availed promptly and comprehensively of the opportunities provided by the ICT strand of the project, arranging to have most of their staff members participate in a series of workshops. In schools where the participation was greatest, teachers were grouped in co-operating teams, which helped to sustain learning efforts between one workshop and the next. In other schools the take-up was more gradual, though with substantial interest shown from the start. In others still, the enthusiasm of a small number of teachers was matched by a 'techno-wariness' among others, and efforts had to be given to illustrating how the adept use of ICT, far from displacing or relegating the teacher, could enhance the rapport between teachers and students; not least by involving the students in more wholehearted and more co-operative ways in learning. These efforts were more often than not successful, though not all-at-once, and it soon emerged that there were different patterns of engagement, or different rhythms of engagement, in the different schools. From a practical point of view this worked out well, as it made it more possible for attentions to be concentrated on different schools at different times.

Two approaches, devised as successive phases, were adopted to further the aims of the ICT strand. The first of these was *The Digital Resource*. This enabled participating teachers to become proficient in carrying out targeted web searches for their subjects, including the collecting, storing, using and managing of personalised resource collections for the new approaches they were mastering. The second phase was called *Linking4Learning*. This was designed to encourage investigative teaching and learning and to complement the project's efforts in promoting a range of approaches from the assessment for learning family. During this phase teachers were tutored in using 'Nvu', a user-friendly programme which they would subsequently use with their students for creating and managing interactive websites. One of the main attractions of this was that it stimulated enquiry-based learning in the different school subjects, including a quickening of interest in otherwise uninviting areas of the syllabus and the tailoring of curriculum material to individual circumstances.

In the later stages of the project, and particularly in the final year, participants in the ICT strand increasingly voiced their greater confidence in using web-based resources as a feature of their regular classroom practice, not just in the preparation of lessons. This confidence was reported by teachers in Geography, Music, Home Economics, Business Studies, History, Religious Education, French, as well as in the four original subjects Maths, Science, Irish and English. It included moreover not only the teaching that took place in designated computer rooms but also in conventional classrooms. In the latter cases however, the classroom had to be equipped with a web connection, a computer (desktop or laptop), and a data projector (fixed or portable). In the minority of cases where interactive whiteboards were available in classrooms, teachers reported that students responded enthusiastically and that the possibilities for a richer experience of learning were greatly improved. In the former (i.e. in computer rooms), gains were best when it was possible to place students individually or in pairs at terminals and coach them in using interactive sites; for instance in composition or completion exercises in Music, in accomplishing increased familiarity with vocabulary and grammar in German and French, in carrying out rudimentary or more advanced research exercises in Home Economics and in History.

The generally positive nature of teachers' comments on incorporating ICT progressively into their own practice were tempered however by frustrations in relation to the availability and reliability of equipment. For instance, in addition to frequent comments on the unavailability, or the delayed availability of ICT equipment, teachers regularly spoke of having no option but to put groups of students, rather than individuals or pairs, at the terminals in a computer room that were actually working dependably on the day. Teachers were high in their praise of school leaders who were working diligently to provide well equipped and user-friendly ICT learning environments in the schools.

At the close of the project, significant changes in attitudes and practices are evident where ICT in teaching is concerned. Two concluding points can be made on this. Firstly, where teachers have become quite accomplished in using the new technologies with their students, the tenor of their views is that while there may still be a place for the designated computer room in schools of the future, a more progressive policy is to equip each classroom so that it can become a reliable multimedia learning environment. Secondly, where teachers more generally are concerned, the following comment from one teacher provides a good summary of a widely-held view. 'I have come to see much merit in the integration of ICT into teaching, as something that can assist but not replace the teacher. It is a tool, not a panacea. It can assist and enhance the learning experience, it cannot teach. Its use must constitute a component of some lessons. The facilities must be classroom-based and available to the teacher as and when she requires to use them'.

(7) Cultivating teacher networks

Participant teachers warmly refer to the benefits gained as a result of their engagement with the project. For the most part, teachers feel considerably less isolated than a few years ago and speak of their increasing role in sharing ideas and practices with colleagues. In addition to the formal collaborative networks the project instituted, significant numbers of teachers established their own informal groupings. Teachers who previously didn't know each other now contacted each other to seek clarification on ideas exchanged at workshops and also to develop joint presentations or resources. Networks such as these are regarded by teachers as a major benefit of the project. Early in the second year of the project, to promote these informal associations further, a virtual learning facility was set up for any of the projects participants who were keen to avail of it. This allowed teachers to contact each other through a secure web network, thus enabling them to post requests and upload and download digital resources. De-privatising practice to this level, where participant teachers have become at ease in researching and discussing pedagogic practice in front of mixed audiences has, for many, taken significant amounts of time, clarification, trust-building and persuasion. This is understandable, particularly in the light of the prevailing traditions of insulation and isolation we reviewed earlier. The professional learning communities the project sought to build did not merely consist of swapping materials and exchanging activities. They were keenly focused on a sharing of expertise and perspectives on teaching and learning, which helped to develop among the participants a sense of shared responsibility for the *quality* of learning. In this way the informal networks were an opportunity to promote an enhanced sense of professional identity among their members.

Looking ahead now, the question arises as to whether such networks can be sustained and developed further. The networks can be face-to-face or electronic ones, or a combination of both. Either way, and like the informal networks for school leaders mentioned in Chapter 2, they require someone to act as convenor, or co-ordinator, perhaps on a rotating basis, or on a fixed term basis. They also require a home server for the digital learning environment. In the longer term it might be possible for Education Centres to provide these. For the year 2007-08, NUI Maynooth has agreed to continue to provide the 'Moodle' environment that was made available for the project's participants. There are further comments on this issue in Chapter 5.

Chapter 4

Engaging Students in their Own Learning

(1) Overview of main developments

The new approaches to teaching reviewed in the last chapter played a crucial part in promoting the second main aim of the project, that of enabling students to take a more active and responsible hand in their own learning. There are two main aspects to this aim: firstly, changes in the attitudes the students take to their work and in the energies they put into it; secondly, changes in the actual achievements of the students. Notable advances were made in both during the lifespan of the project, though the first aspect is more easily assessed than the second, despite any claims to the contrary. For instance, where students who have previously been at best compliant become enthused about their work with a particular teacher, changes in the learning environment and in work effort become readily noticeable. Even where a small number of students begin to change, this invariably influences others in the class, and initial breakthroughs are usually followed by some gathering of momentum. Where improvements in students' achievements are concerned, teachers themselves can of course assess these through periodic tests and assignments, but it takes a longer time for such improvements to show reliably in national certificate examinations.

The evidence we gathered on changes in students' learning is drawn from two main sources. Firstly, some of the teacher participants in the TL21 project followed the optional accreditation paths. In those cases, as part of their own action research projects, the teachers monitored the changes in attitudes and achievements of students in particular classes selected for close study. In addition, more intensive action research studies were undertaken by three members of the project team. Gains in students' achievements as well as improvements in students' attitudes to learning were recorded in the research projects and in the team members' studies. Secondly, the teacher participants more generally reported any significant improvements in their students' work to fellow participants at workshops and to

41

members of the project team. School Principals and Deputy Principals did likewise. At the conclusion of the project's active phase, video evidence from a representative range of classrooms was presented at the Exhibition and Colloquium held in Maynooth on 14th June 2007. For this overview, the main findings on changes in the quality of students' learning are summarised below. This summary is followed by explorations of some of the strategies used to promote the changes. Then we review the effects of initiatives with ICT on students' learning and the chapter closes with some concise examples of the kinds of advances made in students' learning achievements.

- The use of new teaching and learning strategies – mainly from the assessment for learning family – brought about significant improvements in students' attitudes to their work and to their active involvement in that work.

- Such improvements were also accompanied by marked changes in the classroom learning environment, including a decrease in discipline problems, greater co-operation between students in group-work and pair-work, improved completion of homework and in a few instances by better attendance rates.

- Where teachers persevered with new approaches and monitored their effects closely, significant improvements took place in the achievements of students, most notably in the case of students normally seen as poor achievers.

- Some teachers found that their first attempts in using new approaches were resisted by students. The project's workshops and other informal networking among teachers were found to be valuable opportunities for teachers to share with each other the challenges they were experiencing, and were regarded as a major source of support and encouragement by the teachers.

- The best improvements in students' learning were recorded where teachers began with just one or two changes in approach and subsequently introduced others in a gradual way.

- In a small number of cases teachers reported that the new approaches they tried didn't work, and then did not persevere beyond the initial challenges, despite encouragement from colleagues at workshops. In these instances no appreciable changes took place among the students. In such cases however teachers invariably reported that the predominant cultures in which they had to work, including parental influences in such cultures, were unswervingly conservative and restrictive.

- Where teachers pursued new approaches with students over an extended period, changes in learning environments were sometimes striking, including regular features like a readiness on students' part to ask questions, to venture an answer that might be wrong, to accept ideas and correction from other students, to propose suggestions for project work and homework.

It is important to add a cautionary note here. We have referred briefly above to the point that the new approaches that promoted changes such as those just listed were drawn mainly from the assessment for learning family. Assessment for learning (AfL) has quite rightly received a lot of prominence in educational reform internationally in recent years. Unfortunately however this notoriety has tended to cast it as a panacea (even a quick fix) for some, and something to be dismissed as the latest vogue by others. Needless to say both of these reactions are mistaken, but the real significance of assessment for learning is also bypassed if one sees it mainly as a 'toolkit', or its constituent elements chiefly as a set of skills.   Engaging with new pedagogical approaches, if it is to be something more than a superficial or half-hearted effort on the part of teachers, means gradually opening up to new ways of doing things. Even where one takes on new approach in the hope of a quick fix, one is soon presented with a frank choice: to drop the idea and revert to one's previous methods, or to accept new challenges and encounter the new understandings of one's own work that negotiating such challenges involves. The latter path, as can be gleaned from the summary of evidence above, can lead to meaningful and enduring changes, but for teachers to venture successfully on this path they need regular support – from colleagues, from school leadership and from support agencies outside of the school.

(2) Exploring the changes in students' learning

Having concluded our overview of findings with this word of caution, we will now consider in turn the kinds of new approaches that teaches in the TL21 project took on and the consequences of these initiatives for the quality of learning among students. In making plans for the approaches we would concentrate on, we consulted with staff at the National Council for Curriculum and Assessment, who in recent years have been carrying out projects on AfL in a number of schools settings. As initiatives were progressing in the schools we held a special seminar on AfL in October 2006, hosted by Chris Baker, an international authority on AfL. The TL21 team concentrated on five main AfL approaches with the project's participants. These approaches complement and reinforce each other. The five approaches do not constitute an exhaustive list however, and many of the participating teachers moved beyond these to employ further innovations in their work. In any case, the five approaches, which we will now review in turn, are:

a. Specifying learning intentions and criteria and monitoring the consequences

b. Using questions to enhance learning – 'no hands' and 'wait time'

c. Promoting group-work, peer learning and autonomous learning among students

d. Cultivating self-assessment and peer-assessment by students

e. Strengthening the role of comment and feedback to improve students' learning.

(a) Specifying learning intentions and criteria

As the exchanges between teachers became more informal at the project's early workshops, concerns began to be exchanged more frankly. Notable among these was the concern that teachers themselves were practically doing the learning for many of their students. To address this in an initial way, it was decided to try out the approach called 'specifying the learning intentions and the learning criteria for a lesson'. This approach is based on the belief that students' efforts at learning are likely to be more engaged if they clearly know from the start of a lesson what the main learning goals are and what the criteria are for assessing their own progress towards these goals. The teacher introduces both at the beginning of a lesson with the acronym WALT (what are we learning today) for the contents of the lesson, and WILF (what I'm looking for) to make explicit a few key criteria for assignments in class or for homework. The acronyms themselves can be dispensed with as the students get more familiar with the procedure, but the air of novelty they provide can be helpful in early stages.

Before long teachers began to report that the use of these basic, yet searching approaches stimulated students to became more involved in their own learning. In the early stages this was evident chiefly in students being 'busier', 'more attentive', 'more interested' and 'more alert' in class. Many teachers were surprised that hitherto reluctant students now began to volunteer to get involved in the classwork. They also reported that students started to interact in new ways with each other; ways that were more focused on learning than on exchanging jokes and gossip. Teachers then found that as students got more involved in their own learning, teachers' own role in classrooms began to change. They were no longer 'jumping in', as one teacher put it, to 'assess individual students on the spot' and instead began to listen to the students more thoughtfully. Thus they began to gain a much clearer understanding of what students were actually learning and understanding during a class. Students themselves reported feeling more involved in the learning process. The following are some representative comments from students about the learning intention and criteria for success: 'The criteria for success force me to think about how I can improve'. ... 'Instead of asking the teacher how to do the question, I look up the criteria for success sheet and try and work it out myself'. ... 'I feel I think more about how to improve and that it's my responsibility'. ... 'I really like and enjoy this way of teaching, it helps me understand things more easily'. ... 'It's much easier remembering what I do for myself rather than someone else doing it for me'. Over and over again students commented that they felt more active in class and liked getting involved, 'instead of just sitting there and listening for the whole class'.

Teachers often collaborated with students in working out the criteria and this proved very successful. Building on experiences like this, students became generally less anxious in class. They reported finding it easier to remember their work and consequently they didn't worry as much. However students were keen to point out that the subject being studied, and the level at which they were taking that subject (Foundation, Ordinary or Higher), played a key part in students' own levels of anxiety. For instance, some students who were generally positive about their involvement in class still felt anxious in mathematics class.

Changes in students' achievements developed in an unforced way from their changes in attitude. Teachers who employed learning intentions and learning criteria over an extended period all reported gains in students' achievements. Most notably, completion rates for classwork assignments were higher, and there were gains in understanding and accuracy. Likewise, more thoroughness was evident in homework. These teachers also felt that they themselves began to teach better. Through planning and developing learning intentions and criteria for success, teachers reported that they became progressively clearer themselves about what was to be learned. This made them attend more perceptively to how they would teach a topic and to difficulties in their students' understanding. Students attributed their own higher achievements to the fact that studying was made easier when they had the criteria for success to consult. Students pointed out that 'instead of reading a whole textbook, you consult the criteria for success'. In this way, study took less time, and yet, as one student put it, 'I am taking more in'. The most common response from students was that they now understood better what they had to learn and that this made it easier. One student simply wrote 'Criteria for Success – At last I've got a C'.

(*b*) Using questions to enhance learning

At workshops in the early stages of the project teachers often pointed out that some students rarely or never answer in class. Possible reasons for this were discussed by the teachers and among the chief reasons they came up with were: perhaps the students don't know the answer, or they are not given the time or opportunity to answer, or they may be afraid of giving the wrong answer. Exploring the many uses of questions thus became a focus for critical attention in workshops. As teachers examined their own practices they began to acknowledge that all too frequently the questions used in class were closed ones, leading just to right or wrong answers. This excluded many students from participating, even from thinking further about the question, because they simply concluded that they did not know the right answer. There was a general acknowledgement in the workshops that such questions rarely promoted learning and often sent out negative signals to students.

Arising from this, teachers were keen to know how they could use questioning to encourage greater participation by students. Workshops then concentrated on strategies for creating a safe climate for students to think about questions in the classroom and to venture answers that revealed this thinking to others, even when it might contain errors, or might be on the wrong track. Teachers began to plan more open questions for their lessons: questions to which every student can have some kind of answer; questions which make students think at some length and probe further for solutions or reasons; questions which promote discussion. For instance, such questions may involve showing two objects or pictures, or playing two pieces of music, and asking students to discover in what ways the objects/pictures/music are similar and in what ways they are different. This frequently involved cultivating a 'think, pair, share' approach among the students. In other words, each student thinks of an answer on his/her own, discusses it with a partner and then with a small group. In this way every student is involved.

To encourage active student engagement teachers asked students to write questions about the things they did not know or understand about the topic being discussed. In this approach, each student comes up with a question and contributes it to a small group. Then each group selects one question from their group's list. This is then read out and given to the next group. The next group reads out their question, which is given to another group, and so on until all groups have a question. The groups are then given a set amount of time to discuss their particular question, find out what they can about it, and then answer to the whole class. Such approaches were found to encourage in students the capacity to generate questions of their own, and to raise questions spontaneously about new topics introduced by the teacher.

Teachers began to realise that they could relegate the place of a 'hands up' policy if they asked more open-ended, or exploratory kinds of questions. With this also came the realisation that students needed to be allowed sufficient thinking time, and sometimes discussion time, in order to contribute meaningful answers. In the initial stages many teachers found it very hard to refrain from a 'hands up' approach, or to allow 'wait time' for the students to give considered answers. Moving away from a 'hands up' policy invariably involves a different approach to the exploration of the subject by the teacher and a necessity to come up with open rather than closed questions. In the early stages students, no less than teachers, found it hard to discard the habit of putting their hands up and many students and teachers felt that 'wait time' was somehow showing students up if they did not have an answer. Teachers also found that they tended to supply the answer during 'wait time' themselves. To address these concerns a systematic procedure for random selection was devised. Each student, or pair of students, would be given a playing card, and then a card would be selected at random. The student or pair with that card provided an answer and then chose the next card. This method spread the responsibility to think among all of the students.

Feedback from students revealed a strong consensus that more open questioning builds up their confidence to get involved in class. Students noted that with closed questioning the same people would always put up their hands to answer, while with open questioning everyone was getting a chance. One student summed it up as follows: 'Before, if I didn't know the answer I'd never put my hand up. Now that we don't have to have a right answer I give things my best shot'. Conversely, students who had been in the habit of putting up their hands felt that they were now getting a break. Teachers reported that by thinking and planning their questioning and refining the 'wait time' strategy, their students had become far more involved, alert and cooperative in class. Students commented that they felt they were learning more because they were more focused and involved in class: 'I see a lot more work being put into class and homework among my friends and me'. Generally students felt that 'wait time' was so simple, but also so effective, because it encouraged them, without fear of embarrassment, to think for themselves. Students agreed that previously 'someone would just shout out the answer', usually the same few, thus letting everyone else off the hook. Finally, teachers who revised their questioning approaches along these lines commented that they were 'getting on much better' with students. The atmosphere in class had changed, had become more relaxed, with more work being done by students.

(c) Promoting group-work, peer learning and autonomous learning

Although different forms of group work have been common in our primary schools for many years, they have played a minor role in post-primary schools, being largely confined to newer programmes such as the Transition Year and the Leaving Certificate Applied. (ESRI/NCCA 2004). There is a growing awareness however of a necessity for change. The recommendations for post-primary schools contained in the *Chief Inspector's Report 2001-2004* stressed the importance of active and differentiated learning strategies that encourage students' engagement and independent learning (DES 2005, p.9). The international literature on lifelong learning and 'the learning society', both in official reports and in critical research studies, also gives prominence to strengthening a capacity to learn independently over the course of one's lifetime

It is clear that post-primary teachers in the main are not ill-disposed towards group work and similar strategies that cultivate a capacity for autonomous learning in students. Many have concerns however that the use of such strategies might lead to too much noise in the classroom, or might aggravate discipline problems.

Mindful of concerns like these, careful preparatory thought was given in workshops to the kinds of learning activities that teachers might engage in with their students to make progress with group work and autonomous learning. As in the case of the learning intentions and criteria for success reviewed in section (b) above, both teachers and students had to be very clear in advance about the purpose of the particular activity or learning game to be used, about the roles of the different participants in the groups various part, and about the rules of procedure. Equally, care had to be taken by teachers in selecting groups – whether to select on the basis of likely ability to accomplish the activity, as was done on some occasions, or to include students of different abilities in each group. Students, for their part, had to co-operate in groups, often taking on responsibilities that had to be divided among group members. Where this was done on a regular basis, the practice of appointing a group leader was adopted, but with the clear understanding that each member of the group would have to take a turn at some stage as leader. The learning activities for the groups included not only co-operating on written assignments that might normally be given as class exercises to test comprehension that students would complete individually. They also included tasks like composing short dialogues (in language teaching), devising questions that might then be passed on to another group, tackling such questions received from another group, finding out further information from a few essentials furnished by the teacher, and completing portfolios. Inter-school group activities included competitions like *Tráth na gCeist* in Irish, *Game 24* in Mathematics, and the *Linking4Learning* competition in ICT.

The student's comments on their experiences with groupwork are particularly illuminating and it is worth providing an illustrative range of them here. The first of these is a somewhat negative reaction, voicing a view held by some of the more academic, or individually occupied students, especially in the earlier stages: 'Group-work consumes too much time, which could be better used in the class'. Comments like the following however were much more common: 'Yes, she comes around to our groups and she has more time to explain to us because we are all in groups and she explains to four people at a time'. ... 'I feel more involved in the class because the teacher asks the group instead of picking on one person'. ... 'It changes the way you learn because you are not just helping yourself, you are also helping the people in your group'. ... 'I feel less anxious and I'm not afraid that I won't know the answer, because the group is working with you'. A memorable comment from one of the teachers, heartily supported by colleagues, was: 'After five weeks of doing groupwork the students did not want to return to a class where the teacher stood at the front and they, the students, worked individually in their desks'.

(d) Cultivating self-assessment and peer-assessment by students

To practice self-assessment and peer assessment successfully, students need some familiarity with criteria of learning and some practice in dealing with them. This means that self-assessment and peer-assessment should ideally be introduced at a later stage than the more basic strategies of clarifying learning intentions and learning criteria. In fact they are a natural progression from these. In some cases where teachers introduced a self-assessment approach without familiarising the students beforehand in the use of learning intentions and learning criteria, they found that some of the marking was done inaccurately, with consequent complaints by students and other negative effects. In most cases however teachers' initiatives in promoting self-assessment and peer-assessment brought marked benefits to the students' learning, as the comments reported below from the students show. These initiatives ranged from the marking of simple assignments by First Year students to the use of a Leaving Cert Honours marking scheme by students to mark their own work. A representative sample of comments by students on their experiences with self-assessment includes the following: 'When I correct my own work I understand better where I went wrong'. ... 'It's better than the teacher announcing it [a mistake] to the whole class'. ... 'Because I have to figure out my mistakes for myself I'm learning more'. ... ' It's good to see where I can gain or lose marks'. ... 'You can see for your self how you're getting on'.

Two modified forms of self-assessment by students, in both cases not involving the giving of marks or grades, were used extensively by teachers in the project. More precisely, they combined self assessment with the development of autonomous learning. The first of these was an adaptation of a 'traffic lighting' approach and the second was an approach called 'Predict, Observe, Explain'. Teachers adopted the 'traffic lighting' approach both for classwork and homework. In this procedure green, amber and red cards, or stickers, or markers, are used by students to identify points that they don't understand (red), that they understand to some extent (amber), or that they understand well (green). The teacher's attention is drawn in particular by red or amber indicators and thus the teacher's follow-up efforts in clarifying difficulties can be more targeted. From the students' perspective, the use of traffic lighting invariably brings them into a closer involvement in their own learning, and a continual assessment of the results of their own efforts. The feedback from students who have engaged in the use of traffic-lighting regularly includes comments like: 'My grades have improved'; 'It has changed the way we're learning'; 'I'd like other teachers to use this method'.

The POE strategy involves students predicting the outcome of a demonstration or experiment, committing themselves to a possible reason for their prediction, making an observation, and finally explaining any discrepancies between their prediction and observation. Whether used individually or in collaboration with other students, POE tasks stimulate students to explore and justify their own individual ideas, especially in the prediction and reasoning stage. If the observation phase of the POE task shows up some conflict with a student's initial prediction, attention then becomes centred on reconstructions and revisions of initial ideas are possible. Teachers found that carrying out POE in a co-operative way (dividing class into groups) was even more productive than getting students to use it on an individual basis. In adapting the strategy for group use, students write down their individual predictions first (self-assessment), then review individual predictions with the group (peer-assessment), before offering their collective prediction to the teacher. Students' comments on the use of POE include: 'Experiments are now more interesting'. ... 'We don't worry now about having to get the right answer'. ... 'We learn more about the concepts behind the experiment'. Teachers add comments like: 'Students enjoy practical work more using POE; they have a sense of ownership of the experiment'.

(*e*) **Strengthening the role of comment and feedback to improve students' learning**

In returning homework or other assignments to students, teachers normally give a mark or grade and sometimes accompany this with short comments. International research studies in recent decades have found however that conventional forms of marking frequently fail to offer meaningful guidance on how students' learning could be improved (Black & Wiliam 1998). Another important finding was that where marks and comments are provided, students tend to look at the mark but to ignore the comments, even when these are put in constructive terms. The research studies recommend the use of 'comment-only' marking to address this kind of shortcoming. In 'comment-only' marking, the grade is withheld by the marker and comments are focused on a few key points, but as constructive suggestions for the student to consider.

Quite a number of teachers in the TL21 project tried some form of comment-only marking. Their experiences have substantially borne out the international research findings on the merits of this approach, but these experiences were not without difficulties, especially in the early stages. The following example illustrates some of these initial difficulties, though the difficulties in other cases were less pronounced than this one. The teacher concerned had been in the habit of giving students grades for their work on a regular basis, but then switched to a comment-only procedure. Although the teacher explained the purpose of the new approach to the students, many students were unhappy not to receive grades. Some parents also complained to the teacher about this. The teacher explained to the parents, and to the students, that grades had indeed been recorded for all of the assignments that had been completed, but that the grades had been withheld so that students could concentrate on the feedback in the comments. This would steadily improve their learning, and in due course their grades. The difficulties were largely removed when this rationale was explained to parents and when they understood that grades were at all times recorded and could be available to parents if they sought them. In other schools there were no difficulties of this kind. But the early difficulties in adopting a comment-only approach underline the importance of explaining in advance the rationale for this approach to students, and also to parents.

As time went on, teachers using comment-only marking reported reassuring improvements in students' grades in assignments and tests; for instance greater accuracy, more detail in answers, more evidence of method in approaching a task. The improvements were more marked among students who were under-achievers. Most teachers reported that it was easier to introduce comment-only marking with First Years than with senior students, and that Leaving Certificate students in particular could be quite resistant to its introduction. There was general agreement among teachers however that if comment-only marking were to be successfully introduced with a class in the early stages of post-primary schooling, it could then be continued and developed further as that class moved up through the school. One teacher reported considerable success in introducing an approach that combined the provision of focused comments and grades for a Leaving Certificate class. In this case the teacher put a lot of effort into weaning the students away from their preoccupation with grades and into training them to expect more probing comments as time went on.

The following representative remarks by students illustrate some of the benefits brought about by comment-only initiatives and also some of the attitudes that had to be addressed to secure such benefits: 'With comment-only I had to concentrate more on my mistakes' ... 'You can see where you went wrong' ... 'Good, but I really only care about the marks, or who gets highest in the class' ... 'I prefer to get marks, but I did pay more attention to my mistakes'. ... 'He gave me a comment pointing to exactly what I had to do to improve and that was the big jump'.

Evidence reported by the teachers shows that as students become more at home with the idea of receiving feedback on which they are expected to take action, their capacity to become more autonomous as learners can be seen to improve. Proficiency in handling feedback is also contributed to by the other approaches mentioned above, especially self-assessment and the regular use of learning criteria.

(3) Drawing creatively on ICT to enhance the experience of learning

The account in the previous chapter of the two phases of the ICT strand of the project, the *Digital Resource* phase and the *Linking 4 Learning* phase, explored issues like the initial 'techno wariness' of many teachers, the different pacing and rhythm in the ICT strand, the collaborative nature of the participation of teachers in some schools and the more individual style in others, the question of developing ICT facilities in each classroom or concentrating these in dedicated computer rooms, the importance of the school leadership in cultivating an ICT-friendly learning environment in the school, and not least the boost in confidence on the part of very many teachers who have successfully used new strategies and remain on the alert for new possibilities to enrich the learning of their students. It is this latter aspect that concerns us in this here, and the following points, all of which required teachers and students to work co-operatively in new ways, summarise the main advances achieved in the ICT strand of the project:

- teachers and students creating context-rich digital resources in a range of subject areas; for instance: building web pages for a specific classes in History; recording syllabus-relevant outward-bound activities with digital cameras in Science, Geography and History, for subsequent inclusion into multimedia presentations for recall, review, and examinations-oriented revision;

- students carrying out web-based research activities that develop higher-order skills, specifically in projects in Irish, History, Home Economics, Religious Education, Geography, Business Studies, Science, English;

- using PowerPoint presentations created by the students to enhance oral proficiency in target languages such as Irish and German;

- getting First Year and Second Year students to use selected web sites in a systematic way in order to promote better motivation and achievement in Mathematics classes;

- using in classrooms CD materials that were put together by the TL21 team and that were already experimented with in the project's workshops;

- using multimedia sites to develop deeper understanding of complex syllabus content in Science (DNA), Music (composition), Geography (tectonic plate movement, soil transport in river flows);
- using web-based games for language learning (French, German, Spanish);
- creating and sharing of teaching and learning resources in folders on schools' servers, and made available as hyperlinks on schools' websites.

Students' comments on their involvement in these kinds of learning activities were invariably enthusiastic, and reveal some significant changes that have occurred in styles of learning:

'We got the [history] questions from the class and we made up the multiple-choice game by using everybody's ideas. Our teacher helped us. It's a fun way to revise...making and using the website.'

'It makes Business Studies interesting because a group of us use the CDROM at the computer...we take turns...one of us can fill in any of the bits of information some of the rest us don't know.'

'We work on the harmony exercise in the first part of the class, then we go to the computer room... if you don't play the piano...we can help one another to get the notes right when you [can] hear them on the computer.'

'We did the [science] experiment in our group and when we came back to the computer that had the results on it, we had to figure out how ours was different to the one on the site.'

'We like doing maths on the computer. We ask can we do it everyday!'

'Using the computer to make out our menus for Home Economics allowed us to decorate them and use our imagination.'

'Making the PowerPoint and showing it to the class helped me prepare for my oral.'

For the most part, teachers' observations on their own and their students' use of ICT were also enthusiastic. Where reservations were expressed these invariably focused on the frustrations already mentioned in the previous chapter.

(4) Brief Samples of Students' Achievements

In giving these examples here our purpose is to illustrate succinctly typical gains in students' achievements from four subject areas. Fuller accounts of these and other such achievements have been presented, or are being prepared, as part of postgraduate research theses in the university and may be published as research papers in due course.

First example: A teacher of English gradually introduced a range of new active learning approaches with a lower stream Second – Year class in a class in a rigidly streamed Junior Cycle. At the beginning of the year it was felt that only four of the thirty students in the class could attempt a Higher Level paper. As the result of the teacher's innovations however every student in the class sat the Higher Level paper and every student achieved a C grade or higher in the Junior Certificate examinations.

Second example: A teacher of English introduced some assessment for learning approaches with a Fifth Year class where the quality of engagement and the quality of homework were poor to very poor. After persisting with a the new approaches for some weeks the teacher reported a marked difference in the students' level of attainment. Quality of homework improved steadily and students also became markedly more engaged in classroom work.

Third example: A teacher of science sought to discover if using a constructivist approach with First Years would improve grades in science tests. He taught one class using the 'traditional' approach he used prior to his involvement in the TL21 project. He taught the second class using a constructivist approach, where students had to contribute to discovering solutions. Both classes were given three identical tests over the course of this period. this period. The class average for the students taught using constructivist approach was higher than that for the other class in all three tests

Fourth example: Another science teacher taught one Fifth Year Biology class using a conventional approach and taught a comparable class using PowerPoint presentations with animation and video clips embedded. Both classes were given test questions taken from Leaving Certificate papers. Again, sequential tests were used during this innovation and it was found that class average for class taught using ICT approach reached 62%, a full 11% higher than other class.

Fifth example: A teacher of Mathematics used a range of active learning methodologies with a Higher level mathematics class over the two years of the Senior Cycle. Most of the students did not perform well in the Pre-Leaving Examinations and the teacher became very concerned. The teacher discussed these concerns with the Principal, who encouraged the to persist with the active learning methodologies. Both teacher and Principal were pleased to report that when the Leaving Certificate results were released the students had excelled themselves. They attribute the students' success clearly to the active learning approaches

Sixth example: A teacher introduced self-assessment with a Second Year mixed ability Mathematics class and sustained this approach for two years. A class of this kind in the school normally has about 25 students, with only 15 or 16 completing the Higher Level course. However after two years of using self-assessment only four students did not complete the Higher Level course; a significant achievement for the students and the school. The teacher and students attributed this to the self-assessment methods that had been used over the two years.

Seventh example: A teacher of Irish assessed the oral skills of a Fourth Year group in First Term using an interview test, and then introduced used group work to promote an improvement in oral skills among the students. The teacher tested the students again in Third Term using the same instrument. An average improvement of 15% was recoded in the students' performance. Instances of error also decreased and thee was more detail evident in the answering of questions. Most of the students showed a greater willingness to communicate in the second test and a reduction in unease to speak.

Eighth example: A teacher of Irish had a Second Year class who had all failed the end-of-year exam in Irish in First Year. The teacher introduced a range of active learning approaches to promote greater learner autonomy among the students and continued with these approaches during Second Year. At the end-of year exam in Second Year, all but two of the students passed, with increases of 15% to 20% in grades in almost all cases.

Chapter 5

Supporting and Sustaining Good Practice in Continuing Professional Development

(1) Overview

Research and Development initiatives like the TL21 project provide valuable opportunities to try out new ideas and practices in a representative sample of school settings. These include ideas and practices from international research, but also ones that are home-grown. Such projects are essentially exploratory. They experiment with new forms of continuing professional development (**CPD**) for teachers, but they are in no sense a substitution for the work of the national support agencies involved in such work. Where they take an action research approach, as distinct from a more traditional academic one, critically important relationships can be built, not only with teacher practitioners and school leaders, but also with educational support agencies, managerial bodies, teacher unions and other major partners in education. In the case of the TL21 project, the mutual feedback and incremental learning that such an approach embodies has sought to advance a research-informed consensus on key issues and to highlight promising directions for educational policy. As distinct from creating knowledge in a mainly academic sense, projects like this can advance the education community's understanding of what works well and what doesn't; of the practices that are more worthy of practitioners' time and effort.

In addition to a plentiful international literature on teacher development, four important official documents, two international and two Irish, have been published in recent years that are relevant to teacher education in the Irish context. These are: (a) the OECD report *Teachers Matter: Attracting Developing and Retaining Effective Teachers* (OECD, 2005); (b) *Teachers Matter: Country Background Report for Ireland* (Coolahan 2003); (c) a shorter document from the European Commission, titled *Common European Principles for Teacher Competences and Qualifications* (European Commission 2005); (d) an evaluation report on the impact of the Second Level Support Service in

Ireland titled: *Cultivating Professional Growth: An Emergent Approach to Teacher Development* (Granville, 2005). All four documents stress the necessity for teachers to be highly qualified in their subject areas, to be highly accomplished in their communicative capabilities – including interpersonal and ICT capabilities, and to have a good understanding of the social and cultural dimensions of education. These documents are also replete with recommendations, as is the international research literature with arguments, that teacher education must be clearly placed within the context of lifelong learning. As the European Commission document, *Common Principles* succinctly puts it: '[T]eachers' professional development should continue throughout their careers and should be supported and encouraged by coherent systems at national, regional and/or local level, as appropriate.' (European Commission 2005, p.3).

The earlier chapters of our report have hopefully shed some new light on this national, regional and local context in the case of Ireland. Rather than repeat what is said elsewhere in the report, we will concentrate our attentions here on those forms of continuing professional development that proved most fruitful during the lifetime of the TL21 project. We believe the project's experience in working with teachers and school leaders has yielded some ideas that are particularly promising for teacher development as a form of lifelong learning.

(2) Continuity and ownership in professional development

In the Introduction we drew attention to a necessity to distinguish between three main kinds of continuing professional development for the teaching profession: those focusing respectively on the needs of the system, the needs of the school and the needs of the individual teacher. Until recently, provision in Ireland concentrated chiefly on the first of these, the needs of the system. The term INSET, or more simply 'in-service', was much more common than the term CPD, and the term 'in-service' itself became primarily associated in the minds of teachers with the needs of the system. Provision was mainly through *delivery* formats using presentations as distinct from *participatory* formats through workshops and seminars. At post-primary level, in-service

61

events were concerned chiefly with new developments in the syllabus for particular courses or with the introduction of new programmes. In addition, in-service occasions were for the most part once-off events, with no apparent connection between one event and the next.

When the TL21 project's workshops with teachers commenced, there were expectations on the part of many of the participating teachers that these would follow the in-service formats with which the teachers were already familiar. We have described in Chapter 3 above how the early workshops gave their first energies to eliciting from teachers expectations of a different kind. These latter were expectations that arose from specific issues in the teachers' own practice that they were happy to work on. Such work was initially undertaken through sharing perspectives with colleagues from other schools and through taking away a few ideas on which they might work on in their own schools. The workshops were designed as scheduled events within a developmental sequence and remained focused on relevant teaching and learning issues from the participants' schools and classrooms. In between workshops, participants engaged in new initiatives in their own schools and classrooms and in discussions with colleagues, ideally with critical friends, on how these initiatives were working in practice.

Chapter 3 has explored in some detail the momentum that gathered through these workshops and the enduring benefits for their teaching and learning work that teachers began to report. At this point however our purpose is to identify the main features that contributed to the success of the teachers' workshops, and also to the success of the seminars for school leaders as professional development exercises. Four features in particular are worth emphasising.

(1) Active participation: The workshops were designed and convened by members of the TL21 project team in on-going consultation with the participants. From the start they were of an interactive nature. As time went on moreover participants themselves took a more active hand in both the design and the hosting of the workshops.

(2) Meaningful collaboration: As trust was built up participants exchanged more frankly their perspectives and concerns on

teaching and learning issues, arising mainly from their experience within their schools and classrooms. This strengthened a sense of mutual support and shared responsibility among participants. This sense was encouraged also by strategies such as the 'Critical Friend' and by the participants' access to their own virtual learning environment, using the ICT facility 'Moodle'.

(3) Clearly defined tasks: These tasks arose from the specific workshop theme (or themes), and were of two kinds: tasks to be carried out during the workshops and tasks to be carried out by participants between one workshop and the next.

(4) Continuity: The workshops were designed as scheduled events within a developmental sequence. Each workshop had particular contributions to make to the progressive development of specific capacities on the part of the participants.

(5) Feedback: This included (a) feedback (evaluation) to the workshop convenor after each workshop and (b) feedback (progress reports) by participants each other during the course of each workshop on teaching and learning initiatives being undertaken by participants in their own schools.

From the outset the project team were keen to gather data on the long term impact of the workshops on: (a) the teachers' own classroom experiences; (b) the students' learning; and (c) the exchange of pedagogical ideas and practices within and across different subject departments in schools.

Features such as the five above have cultivated collegial environments that yielded marked advances in participants' sense of professional identity and a new awareness of workshop-style groupings as learning communities in which practitioners have a decisive sense of ownership. The research literature (e.g. Wenger, 1998; Rose & Reynolds, 2006) highlights the importance of such ownership, but also stresses the point that it is difficult to achieve it through 'once-off' in-service events or through a format that relies more on lecture style presentations than on participatory sessions.

(3) Looking ahead: four key points

There is a strong case to be made, not least from the evidence we have found during the TL21 project, for giving a much more central place in Ireland's provision for CPD to workshops with features such as these. This is particularly true of provision for the needs of the school as a learning community and the needs of teachers of individual subjects at post-primary level. In the latter case of course, there is sometimes a considerable overlap with the capacity needs of the post-primary system as a whole. From our contacts with the various support agencies that have developed or expanded in recent years, it is clear that they are keen to strengthen their involvement in workshops of this kind. Such agencies include the SDPI, LDS, SLSS, and not least the Education Centres. They also include non-government bodies like the subject associations and the Network of School Planners of Ireland. Our contacts with the managerial bodies and the teacher unions have also established that they are supportive of the goal of an expanded CPD provision marked by participation, collaboration, continuity and feedback.

How the expansion of the support services might best be organised to accomplish this goal raises a host of strategic and organisational issues. We do not see it as appropriate for us to make specific recommendations as to how these services might best be organised for the future. The report *Cultivating Profess-ional Growth* alluded to a little earlier (Granville 2005) has done just that. There are also the many insights furnished by the *Teachers Matter: Country Background Report for Ireland*, and the recommendations made by both the OECD and the European Commission. What we can do here, and are indeed keen to do, is stress a few key points, in fact four, informed by our recent practical researches, that need to be continually to the fore if Ireland is to develop a CPD provision for its teachers which is as good as any in the world.

The first of these is that there are decisive gains to be made if the continuing professional development of teachers, particularly the active forms of it reviewed in this report, is to be raised to a key priority in Ireland's *National Development Plan 2007-2013*. As we mentioned in the Introduction, the importance of this came home to us not at the start of the project, but as we saw the transformations that took place in learning environments where teachers and students found new and energetic ways to learn together. The other side of this of course is that a failure to grasp the opportunity to make CPD a national development priority is to perpetuate a mistaken view of teachers as being more functionaries than innovators.

The second point is the necessity to get rid of the lingering idea, and not just among teachers themselves, that continuing professional development is an 'add on' rather than an integral part of the teacher's occupational life. Among the implications of this are that the concept of 'teacher release' for CPD activities has to be consigned to the past and replaced by CPD as series of scheduled events in a coherent sequence, provided for in the normal school calendar. This does not rule out of course CPD activities that might be undertaken in the teacher's own time. It also leave open that accreditation of CPD might be considered for activities engage in during the normal working week or outside of it. (The next chapter suggests that accreditation might be available for certain *kinds* of CPD activities as distinct from others; not on the basis of whether they are carried out in one's own time or during the normal working week.)

The third point arises from the two previous ones and concerns the maximising of productive energies in developing a coherent, dynamic CPD provision. It arises from heartening work practices that we observed in some of the support agencies, and with which we were happy to be able to join our own efforts from time to time. Put simply, this point is that where the work of a particular body or agency has shown its thinking to be strategic and co-operative, and its practices to be innovative and fruitful, it makes good sense to build on emergent traditions of accomplishment and concentrate resources accordingly.

The fourth point concerns informal networks for continuing professional development. These often grow out of teachers' involvement in formal initiatives, whether through the work of the support agencies, including Education Centres, or through participating in postgraduate courses, or in projects like the TL21 project. They can also arise less formally through the activities of the subject associations. The success of informal networks is usually associated with the presence, in at least some of its members, of an enhanced capacity in teaching and learning and a lively *esprit de corps*, keen to develop such capacity further. They are essentially voluntary bodies however and in order to increase and multiply, and especially to become enduring features of the educational landscape on a regional basis, the networks need a clear means of sustenance. This means not only financial sustenance, but also the services of a convenor or co-ordinator who might act for a fixed term before handing over to a colleague who might do the same. Each network also needs a home, physical in the first instance, and in some cases also an electronic home for a virtual learning environment. From our own experience in the project, it is clear that the Education Centres we have been most regularly in contact with, as well as the Curriculum Development Unit of CDVEC, seem continually willing to provide such homes.

Whatever eventual structures are adopted, we have good reason to believe that if the expansion of CPD provision in the period ahead is guided by key ideas like the four we have just discussed here, that provision can become a model for other countries to follow.

Chapter 6

Accreditation

(1) A survey of issues

The TL21 project provided an accreditation track as an option for any of the participants who were interested in linking their work on the project to obtaining a postgraduate award from the National University of Ireland. Following discussions with teachers' representatives, managerial bodies and the university authorities, an accreditation structure with three stages was designed. Stage 1 was a preparatory year, during which the candidate (e.g. teacher, Deputy Principal or Principal) put together a portfolio on a particular initiative he or she was undertaking in the school. An analytic account of the progress of the initiative (8,000 words) had to be presented in the portfolio. The candidates' work on their portfolios was monitored by members of the TL21 project team at Maynooth, but candidates were not registered students of the university during this preparatory year. An assessment of the portfolios took place at the end of the year and candidates who achieved a standard equivalent to Second Class Honours Grade 1 (H.2.1), or 1ˢᵗ Class Honours (H.1), were deemed eligible to proceed to Stage 2. In Stage 2, candidates became registered students of the university for a year and completed an action research project of 8,000 words for the award of a Higher Diploma in Innovative Learning. Candidates had to choose as their research topic some aspect of their practice in school, dealing with teaching and learning, on which specific initiatives were being taken. Students who received a grade of H.2.1 or H.1 in the Higher Diploma could, if they wished, forgo the award of the diploma and thus become eligible to proceed to Stage 3. This was a further year's study during which an M.Ed. dissertation of 30,000 words had to be completed. Again, the research for the dissertation had to focus on developments in the school's learning environment in which the candidate was actively involved.

Special seminars on action research methodology were held in Maynooth for the accreditation candidates during each of the three stages and further contacts took place between the candidates and the supervisors of their research projects or dissertations. The accreditation candidates were also required to attend in full the workshops and seminars for the project's ordinary participants. The actual research work for accreditation was carried out in the schools however, rather than on campus. In this connection it should be stressed that the accreditation candidates were not being trained as educational researchers with a capacity to gather and analyse sophisticated quantitative data. Rather the emphasis was on cultivating a capacity to evaluate in a discerning way their own practice and that of their colleagues. The accreditation candidates might thus become more accomplished in enhancing the learning environments of their own classrooms, and more widely of their own schools. They might also become better placed to take an active hand in developing learning networks with colleagues from other schools, including face-to-face networks and electronic networks.

The focus on strengthening communities of learning within the participants' own schools marked a departure from the more traditional kind of research work completed for postgraduate awards in university education departments. This includes a departure from the recent generation of qualitative work which has yielded rich findings from schools but has not involved the researcher as an active participant in the research. Although the pursuit of postgraduate qualifications in education has contributed significantly to the professional development of Ireland's teachers in the last few decades, the benefits have predominantly accrued to the individual teacher. There have of course been benefits to schools and to the education system more widely, but these have been more indirect than direct; for instance, through the accumulated actions of a teaching force that becomes increasingly well-versed in the findings of research on good educational practice.

The assessment criteria for all three stages of the accreditation track were designed to include teachers as subjects of their own research and bring about significant changes within and beyond their own classrooms. These criteria sought specific kinds of evidence in the completed research projects. For instance, at Stage 1 the criteria included requirements like the following: evidence of sustained critical reflection on one or more selected aspects of one's own teaching; evidence of progressive engagement with one's critical friend and of the key benefits to one's teaching resulting from such engagement; evidence of regular use in classroom settings of ideas for innovative teaching and learning; evidence of a capacity to pursue independent research on one's practice, availing of pertinent research sources in an initial but discerning way. More advanced criteria were added during Stage 2 and Stage 3. For example, the Stage 3 criteria included: evidence of an important initiative, or series of initiatives, currently under way to influence the wider learning environment of the school; evidence of a critical engagement with issues of quality in learning, particularly as these feature in the school's development planning; evidence that students have become proficient in taking an active hand in their own learning, and of contributing in creative ways to the learning environment(s) of the school; evidence of promising ideas for practice that can be recommended more widely. Details of the accreditation criteria are provided in Appendix 6 and Appendix 7.

Of the project's initial 150 participants, 24 entered the accreditation track in 2004-05 and a further 6 entered in 2005-06. Due to the limited timescale of the project, no more than two intakes could be accommodated. Of the original intake, 12 completed all three stages and received their M.Ed. degrees by the end of 2006-07. A further 4 of this group are currently working on their M.Ed. dissertations. Of the remaining 8 candidates, 4 left the accreditation track after obtaining the Higher Diploma in Innovative Learning and 4 left it before completing the diploma. Of the 6 candidates who entered in 2005-06, 3 are currently carrying out their M.Ed. studies and 2 more are also likely to complete the M.Ed. within a year or two. The remaining candidate left the accreditation track after completing the Higher Diploma in Innovative Learning. All-in-all, of the 30 candidates who joined the accreditation track, 20 or so are likely to complete the M.Ed., a further 5 candidates left the accreditation track after obtaining the Higher Diploma and the remaining 5 candidates left it before obtaining the diploma.

Some pertinent issues for continuing professional development arise from this data, and more generally from this experiment in accreditation and new course development. Looking first at the participation rate in the accreditation track, the overall rate was 20% (30/150). This is a respectable rate, though a bit lower than what we originally envisaged. We had expected the second intake to be lower than the first; that it might be about half of the first, rather than the quarter that it turned out to be. We pursued enquires on this issue (informally because of the relatively small numbers whom it concerned) and gleaned some revealing information from participants who either didn't join the accreditation track or who left it before completing Stage 2 (i.e. before obtaining the Higher Diploma in Innovative Learning).

The more salient points in this information include the following five: cost, duration, workload, changes in school circumstances and changes in personal or family circumstances. In relation to cost, the funding arrangements for the TL21 project made possible a subsidy of €1,000 in each case towards the fees for the Higher Diploma in Innovative Learning and the M.Ed. There were no fees for the preparatory year, as the participants at that stage were not registered students of the university. Despite these allowances, a few participants who were keen to pursue accreditation indicated they were not in a position to do so for reasons of cost. In relation to duration, a few participants declared that the three-year timescale for the accreditation track was too long and asked if it could be reduced to two. This would mean getting rid of the preparatory year and doubling the assessment requirement for the Higher Diploma year. In view of the fact that entrants to the Higher Diploma are required to demonstrate a proven capability to carry out action research, this entry requirement would exclude a larger number of candidates than the few who found the three years too long. In relation to workload, some participants who either didn't join the assessment track, or who joined and left it, found the workload too heavy. The workload in this instance was related very closely to the assessment criteria. It involved just one assignment at each stage, but of greater depth in Stage 2 and of greater depth and extent in Stage 3. The difficulties mentioned by these who found the workload too heavy raise the question of a non-university accreditation route, possibly with a larger number of less demanding assignments, to be completed over a longer period.

70

This question is considered in more detail in the second section of this chapter. Many candidates mentioned changes in school circumstances as a factor in seeking an extension to their registration, and a few mentioned it as a factor in not continuing with accreditation. Such changes usually meant a marked increase in an accreditation candidate's day-to-day responsibilities in the school, or an inability to find a critical friend to replace a departed colleague who had previously played that role. Finally, changes in personal and family circumstances affected quite a number of the project's participants. These were more likely to lead to delays however (i.e. requests for extensions) than to candidates leaving the accreditation track.

(2) Two forms of accreditation

Arising from the survey of issues in the first section of the chapter, closer examination is called for now of two main forms of accreditation in continuing professional development for teachers. The first of these is university accreditation, or accreditation leading to one or other postgraduate qualification. The second is non-university accreditation, typically under the auspices of a professional body such as a statutory Teaching Council. We shall deal with each of these in turn.

Taking university accreditation first, a survey of the dissertation topics for M.Ed. degrees over the last three decades in Irish universities shows some interesting developments. In the eighties for instance, topics attracting the most frequent attention included: school management, curriculum development, subject teaching methodologies, gender issues, educational policies and structures, educational disadvantage, disabilities and special needs (ESAI, 1992). Quantitative studies were the most frequent, though qualitative studies were on the rise and qualitative aspects such as structured interviews featured increasingly in otherwise quantitative studies. Topics dealing with teaching and learning issues were strongly represented, but the predominant emphasis was on establishing and reviewing research findings, as distinct from actively bringing about change through the conduct of the research. This remains the case even where the studies employed more qualitative than quantitative approaches. In recent years action research approaches have made significant headway among Ireland's postgraduate students in education, though more so in research studies on primary than on post-primary schools. Action research here includes not only bringing about changes in practice through the conduct of the research, but also the involvement of the researcher in this process: the researcher as a central participant as distinct from the researcher as an outsider. The research pursued by those in the accreditation track of the TL21 project was exclusively action research in this fuller sense.

The field of educational research is a very wide one and the diversity of research themes pursued in Irish universities to date indicates varying degrees of relevance to the professional development of teachers – ranging from quite marginal to central relevance. Mindful of this, particular care was taken by the TL21 project team in drawing up the criteria for each of the three stages of the accreditation track. Fortunately, some pioneering work had been done by the General Teaching Council in Scotland in elucidating and refining criteria of assessment for professional development, and our early work on designing the accreditation structure for the TL21 project involved a detailed study of the Scottish system. A question arose for us however as to whether the specification of precise assessment criteria might lead to the accreditation track of the project being 'assessment driven', and to a conformist as distinct from an innovative emphasis in the research work carried out by the teacher participants. On investigating this further we concluded that a possible difficulty could be turned to advantage, specifically if the criteria were to be articulated not as measurable outcomes but as requirements for various kinds of evidence, as we have pointed out in the first section of this chapter (e.g. evidence of sustained critical reflection on one's own practice, of working closely with colleagues, of using innovative approaches in teaching and so on. See also Appendix 6 & 7). In this way the criteria would encourage precisely the professional attitudes and practices that identify teachers as the authors of their own work.

The work carried out by the teachers in the accreditation track has been highly praised by the university's external examiner for the M.Ed. in Innovative Learning and the Higher Diploma in Innovative Learning. The developmental nature of this research work, together with its high quality, have clearly served the project's aims well and offer many promising guidelines for the linking of continuing professional development to the earning of postgraduate awards. As we suggested in the final paragraph of the first section of this chapter, there are some issues that need further consideration in advancing such linkages in the future. These include issues of cost, duration, workload, the amount and sequencing of tuition sessions, and not least the balance between off-campus and on-campus work. Fully modularised postgraduate courses might make headway in dealing with most of these issues by allowing candidates to work at their own pace, for instance by allowing the flexibility to take a number of modules at a time or just one module at a time. This kind of flexibility would inevitably mean some changes to the nature and scope of the larger research assignments that are currently pursued in such courses, particularly the dissertation for the M.Ed. degree. It might also require more flexible registration and fee structures for students who pursue the modularised courses. Finally, a further important issue to be mentioned here is determining the place of university-accredited courses within a national professional development framework established by a statutory Teaching Council.

A statutory Teaching Council might also play a leading role in the second main form of accreditation, namely non-university accreditation. Frameworks for professional development that have been established in other jurisdictions (e.g. Scotland, Wales,) have furnished opportunities for teachers to link a sustained involvement in professional development activities to the attainment of new kinds of credentials. These latter include 'the standard for Chartered Teacher' (for teacher practitioners) and 'the standard for School Headship' (for school leaders) (www.gtcs.org.uk, www.gtcw.org.uk). In addition to accomm-odating non-university routes of accreditation, a noteworthy feature of such frameworks is a provision for consultation and review in the light of developments. The Chartered Teacher idea as it works in Scotland and Wales provides for promotion to advanced standing within the teaching profession without drawing practitioners away from teaching and into management. Both systems also allow for non-university as well as university routes to Chartered Teacher. A non-university route (sometimes called portfolio route) to would require a candidate to prepare a comprehensive portfolio on his or her professional development activities over a certain minimum period of time and submit the portfolio for assessment to the appropriate Teaching Council. The preparation of the portfolio would be guided by the relevant criteria specified by the Teaching Council. Although such criteria might require the production of evidence by the candidate of an extensive range of accomplishments, this would not involve the undertaking of the kinds of written assignments that are central to university postgraduate research. Evidence of the extent of a candidate's participation in professional development activities, including face-to-face workshops and electronic workshops, could be included in the portfolio. So also could evidence of the practical fruits of such participation, under a number of pertinent headings.

Our experience in the TL21 project suggests that some participants who find a university route to accreditation of CPD unsuited to their needs might find a non-university route attractive, particularly if it allowed for a longer period of time in putting together a portfolio, or other combination of elements required. This raises the possibility of advancing to the standard of Chartered Teacher in a number of phases. Pursuing this point further, this kind of accreditation might therefore include some intermediate designations, to mark an individual's progression towards Chartered Teacher.

Frameworks that include university and non-university accreditation routes in continuing professional development have been developed in other countries. While an Irish framework needs to be tailored to Irish requirements and circumstances, knowledge and analysis of developments in such frameworks elsewhere can greatly assist such tailoring, an ensure that the Irish design matches the best available internationally.

Chapter 7

Ideas Worth Considering

Introductory remarks

It is normal to finish a report on a research and development project like this with a chapter on recommendations. Such recommendations are typically addressed to policymakers, especially policymakers who control the flow of financial resources, or who are in a position to influence the flow of resources. In short, government Ministries are the main audience, or target, for such recommendations. We have decided to adopt a somewhat different approach here, chiefly for two reasons. Firstly, while policymakers in the Department of Education and Science will hopefully be among the main readers of this report, we are keen that they would be part of a much wider readership. This wider readership would include teachers, school Principals and Deputy Principals, statutory bodies and national support agencies in education, managerial bodies, teacher unions, universities and other centres of teacher education, and not least, educational researchers in Ireland and abroad. A feature of the TL21 project since its inception has been its ongoing conversations with bodies like these. The production of this report, far from concluding these kinds of contacts, will hopefully give them additional impetus and help to place some key issues of common concern in sharper focus. Secondly, while many of the suggestions made in this chapter have implications for funding, and are thus primarily addressed to those who control the purse strings, or who influence that control, the main implications of some of them are for new ways of thinking rather than for greater quantities of money. In one way or another in fact, each of the suggestions seeks to engage the attitudes and practices of *all* education professionals.

Taking both of these reasons together, their significance can be illustrated a bit more by recalling a visit to the project in September 2005 by a delegation from the European Union, representing nine member states. The visitors met the project team and some of the participating teachers, including school Principals and Deputy Principals. They were clearly impressed by the project's progress to date, and not least by the large network of contacts the project team had established with national educational agencies. Mindful of the rifts that can become established between researchers and policymakers, the EU delegation commended the project's efforts to avoid this and urged that no opportunity should be lost to build a 'research-informed consensus' on the key issues the project was addressing. In building such a consensus, which has strengthened since 2005, we were keen however to avoid the danger of 'consensualism' (i.e. a concurrence among dominant voices that marginalises or excludes others), and we hope we have largely succeeded in this.

The suggestions that follow under each of the headings below arise in the first instance from carefully monitored initiatives in the cultural circumstances of Irish secondary schooling, and secondly from what we have learnt from the sharing of emergent insights and lesson with colleagues outside of the project's immediate participants.

1. Teachers as authors of their own work

The evidence presented throughout this report, but particularly in Chapter 3, shows that once initially successful inroads are made on the insulation and isolation of teachers in Irish post-primary schools, some exciting if also challenging possibilities open up. Inherited attitudes that cast teachers in a conformist role are often sustained by teachers themselves, and are reproduced by practices that are deeply lodged in school cultures. We felt that tackling such attitudes head-on would in all likelihood lead to defensiveness and conflict. Workshops that take teachers out of their schools however have proved to be particularly helpful here, by providing the teachers with a hospitable climate to discuss issues in the teaching of their subject with previously unknown colleagues on a recurrent basis. As such workshops proceed bigger issues can enter the discussions and most participants reveal substantial advances in their capability to deal with them. Such enhanced capability can be exercised back in the teachers' own schools in at least two crucial ways. Firstly, within their own classrooms, perhaps initially with certain selected classes, teachers begin to introduce innovations that promote more active involvement by the students in learning. The effects of these innovations are monitored so that the teacher can give a telling account (to himself/herself and to colleagues) of what has worked, what hasn't, and why. Secondly, teachers can also exercise their enhanced capability by endeavouring to strengthen subject teams or departments, and by contributing to such meetings in ways that they wouldn't have ventured to do previously. It is important moreover that the school leadership overtly promotes action on both these fronts. In addition to the encouragement such support gives to teachers, it also sends messages to the school as a whole that words alone couldn't do.

There is also a more advanced sense in which teachers can become the authors of their own work. This is when the focus is placed more on whole-school issues than on the work of an individual teacher or subject team. Our experience with the schools in the project has shown that it takes longer to cultivate this more advanced capability. It has also shown that this cultivation calls for nothing so much as an intensifying and broadening of the kinds of co-operative practices that were nurtured by the workshops in the earlier stages of the project. Increasingly however, the location for cultivating this more advanced capability becomes more the school than the workshop, though informal exchanges between teachers, whether through critical-friendly deliberations in schools or in local professional development networks, also play a key part. A prime example of the exercise of this more advanced capability on a teacher's part is the hosting of a workshop at a whole-school seminar, such as the 'rotation seminars' described in Appendix 5.

In brief, if cultures of professional insulation and isolation of teachers are to yield to ones that strengthen teachers as the authors of their own work, careful attention needs to be given to the kinds of professional development activities that are most conducive to bringing this about. We have found that activities that embody features like those we considered in Chapter 5 are particularly promising. These features are: active participation, clearly-defined tasks, purposeful collaboration, continuity and feedback. For ease of reference we have provided a one-page summary on these features in Appendix 8.

2. Students as active learners

In the introduction to this report we quoted the OECD finding that two-thirds of Irish fifteen-year-olds declared that the were 'frequently bored' in school. Teachers' experiences with the range of approaches considered in Chapter 4 show however that there are ways of tackling such boredom, or low motivation more generally, among students. Apart from a minority of negative comments on comment-only marking from some senior students following Higher Level courses, the tenor of students' observations on the new forms of learning in which they became engaged is very encouraging. Many teachers admitted that they were agreeably surprised by students' willingness to share more of the burden of work in the classroom, and to follow through with more sustained efforts in their homework. This kind of surprise marks a welcome shift of perspective on the part of teachers; a change of mindset – even a change of heart – that enables them to perceive things that they previously disregarded or overlooked. In short, it enable them to learn in new ways *with* their students.

A more active involvement by students in their own learning over a sustained period also led to higher achievements in tests and examinations, and particularly so among students described as less academic. The point to stress here is that such higher achievement is the natural product of something intrinsic, namely a higher quality of educational experience on the part of the students. It should not be confused with the increases in marks and grades that are driven chiefly by extrinsic factors, such as pressures to compete for higher positions on league tables, including unofficial or unacknowledged league tables.

In a few instances changes in the quality of student's learning, occurred in Leaving Certificate classes, as did increases in their examination achievements. This shows that despite the pressures for conformity to older ways that spring from a centralised examination system, there are still many opportunities for teachers to practice creative forms of learning with their students. At the same time, many teachers were reluctant to introduce innovations with examination classes. This was because of a strong belief that the examinations, and the points system for entry to higher education based on it, chiefly rewarded qualities like accurate recall and comprehension. While the points system is likely to remain with us for some time, efforts to reform the Leaving Certificate are continuing. Feedback we have received from teachers over the four years of the project give us good reason to believe that if the Leaving Certificate examination were seen to reward a wider range of accomplishments, including those that flow from active learning approaches, the effects of the points system on schools would be far less constricting. In such circumstances, teachers generally would be much more likely to pursue active learning approaches with Leaving Certificate students.

3. Teachers as a strategic national resource

We have seen that the possibilities for enriching each student's personal development and for advancing a healthy community of learners are greatly enhanced where classrooms become environments of imaginative teaching and active participation by students. We have also seen that such gains move to a higher level and become more widely influential where collaboration between colleagues is successfully cultivated by school leaders. Such productive possibilities and gains are essentially concerned with the intrinsic benefits of education. Where they are fruitfully and widely pursued however, there are very considerable social, cultural and economic consequences; what we might call extrinsic benefits. To put it concisely, imaginative learning environments in schools and colleges are the nurseries for imaginative cultures of innovation in workplaces.

An incisive grasp of this point is of first importance for post-industrial societies (i.e. societies where 'brawn-power' work, and even automated manufacture, is irreversibly declining in proportion to 'brain-power' work). Hence the appropriateness of viewing teachers as a resource of comparable significance for a 'knowledge society' to what reserves of mineral wealth were for an industrial society. Viewed from this perspective, many of the pages of this report can be seen as explorations of how this most valuable of resources can be profitably developed and renewed. The kinds of energies given to date to such renewal, though they have increased in recent years, are still quite minor compared to the strategic importance of the resource itself. It would be a bold departure to move the continuing professional development of teachers from its current place well down the list of priorities in Ireland's *National Development Plan 2007-2013* (see Ch.9) to a place near the top of the list. A comparable bold move was made earlier this decade in the case of higher level research and there is now general agreement that it was a fruitful move. If the initiatives of the TL21 and similar recent development projects can be regarded as experiments of a preliminary kind, the results of these experiments augur well for taking the next big step.

4. School leadership and the demands of administration

The school leadership strand has been central to the TL21 project, although at the beginning, some school leaders who became involved were so busy with administrative work that they considered delegating the conduct of the school's participation in the project to a member of the teaching staff. When they saw that the project itself was in a key sense *about* leadership however, Principals and Deputy Principals endeavoured to make the kinds of adjustments in their own working patterns that would allow their own and their schools' participation in the project to be whole-hearted. In all cases this was difficult to do, and in some cases very difficult. These difficulties are reviewed in some detail in Chapter 2. There we highlighted the point that the learning environments of schools suffer where Principals and Deputy Principals are habitually preoccupied with administration tasks that invariably have to be completed urgently. More specifically, opportunities for teachers to take initiatives with students or with colleagues either do not present themselves, or they do and cannot be properly availed of. Legislation of recent years in Ireland has placed an unprecedented range of responsibilities on the school Principal, many of which are only secondarily connected with the quality of teaching and learning in the school. The international research literature on educational leadership, by contrast, emphasises repeatedly that building and sustaining high quality learning environments is the proper work of school leaders and that time spent on other actions should be continually reviewed in terms of the loss of time to their primary task.

We have also noted in Chapter 2 that some of the participating school leaders in the project worked with commendable perseverance against the administration tide. They used much ingenuity in finding time and opportunities to promote meaningful professional development activities in the school and to enable themselves and their teachers to continue their participation in undertakings like the TL21 project. The efforts involved in this were sometimes all-consuming however, and notwithstanding their fruits they could not be recommended as good practice in any occupation. It is clear that where some progress has already been made in introducing new ides and practices in the schools, recently- appointed Assistant Principals have come to play an increasing part in school leadership, and some school Principals and Deputy Principals have worked closely to further this, availing well of services like **LDS** and **SDPI**. More often however, the work of Assistant Principals involves administration rather than leadership and school leaders themselves need much more time and space to make inroads on this difficulty.

In short, the job of school leaders, and specifically of Principals, has become difficult to the point of crisis in Irish post-primary schools; the essential crisis being the daily press of administration that prevents or frustrates the exercise of specifically educational leadership. If educational leadership is to succeed as it should – and we have seen how well it can – then the bulk of this administration must be undertaken by someone else, with the specific kind of necessary expertise.

5. Different categories of need in continuing professional development

There has been a growing awareness in recent years among the various partners in education of the need to distinguish between the needs of the system, the needs of the school and the needs of individual teachers where continuing professional development is concerned. The drawing of such distinctions helps to clarify thinking in the designing of a coherent professional provision. Such distinctions as sometimes availed of to add to territorial impulses or to secure more resources for one organisation rather than another. Nothing could be further from our purpose in exploring the distinction here. Indeed sometimes there can be a substantial overlap between one of these needs and another, as for instance in the case of the development of fresh capabilities in say, a group of teachers of French in a particular region. Not only are there benefits for the teachers in their work in their own classrooms. There are also benefits for the system, in that there is a general advance in French teaching in the region. There might also be benefits to French learning environments within schools (as distinct from individual classrooms), particularly if teachers begin to share their new approaches in subject teams.

Having said all that however, it is clear that in the past provision for CPD was largely concentrated on the needs of the system, and that the various national support agencies were brought into being to serve these needs. Our experience in liasing with these agencies, particularly the LDS and SDPI, has shown that they are keenly conscious of the different kinds of needs in CPD for teachers, and have been attempting to cater for them as far as their own resources permit. So while it makes good sense to earmark resources to provide adequately for the different kinds of need, this is not necessarily to say that separate bodies have to be established to spend these resources. If one is clear on the particular kind of CPD need that a new initiative is primarily designed to meet, the important question then becomes the adequacy and appropriateness of the means; specifically of the learning activities in which the particular teachers, or school leaders, will participate. Again, it is worth recalling that learning activities with features such as the five described in Chapter 5 (active participation, clearly-defined tasks, purposeful collaboration, continuity, feedback) have been shown to be particularly fruitful. Conversely, the absence of features like these, sometimes even of one of them, can mean that that the professional development needs the new initiative was trying to engage, largely remain unaddressed.

6. CPD as integral or as an 'add-on'

In the months when the TL21 project team were talking to school leaders and teachers about becoming involved in the project, it was surprising to find just how many teachers viewed any kind of formal professional development activity as an 'add on' to an already full workload. In a few instances school Principals themselves, though praising the project's aims, shared this viewpoint and gave it as a reason for declining to participate in the project. At the first workshops moreover, this view was voiced by quite a few teachers. In the course of the project's life however, as workshops and seminars got more to grips with substantial issues, there was a notable shift of perspective. While there were still concerns about finding time for CPD activities like workshops and the note-taking that sometimes needed to be done between workshops, the project's participants came more and more to the view that CPD should be seen as an integral part of the teacher's work. Also revealing is the fact that this view found general agreement in our consultations during the latter half of the project with the national agencies, including the teacher unions. During our early rounds of consultations it had been supported by most agencies, but not all.

Such agreement in principle has important practical consequences that remain to be worked out. Chief among these is the necessity for a negotiated settlement that would enable provision for formal CPD to be accommodated at regular intervals in each school's annual calendar. This has become standard practice in many countries, not all of which reach Ireland's levels of income (i.e. GDP per capita). Some have maintained that such a structure would mean a lengthening of the school year by some five or so days. Others have argued that such days might be designated within the existing totals for the school year. Others still have suggested some combination of both. For our own part we will confine ourselves to two comments on this. Firstly, it is important that a solution to this is found by negotiated agreement, as was the case in Scotland in the McCrone settlement of 2001. In those jurisdictions where such solutions have been imposed, much of the good that they might bring is frustrated, sometimes for years. Secondly, when we compare our own country's provision for CPD with that of countries of roughly comparable population and wealth (e.g. Norway, Finland, Scotland) it is clear that Ireland has much catching up to do. So it is important that energies are given without delay to reaching a solution.

7. Accreditation for CPD

In chapter 6 we gave details of the accreditation pathways that were devised for the TL21 project. These pathways allowed interested participants in the project to proceed in a series of stages to an M.Ed. degree through action research. They also allowed for most of the work to be done on site in the schools. Requirements for attendance on campus were kept to a minimum and extensive use was made of electronic means of communication for tutorial and supervision purposes. Assignments in the earlier stages were focused on selected aspects of participants' professional practice in their own schools. The dissertation for the M.Ed. involved a deeper probing of practice, including the effects of changes brought about in the teachers' own classrooms and in school learning environments more widely. Many valuable insights were revealed by these assignments and dissertations, not only for those who undertook them but also for colleagues with whom the insights were shared in workshops and seminars, including school-based seminars.

While these benefits are to be warmly welcomed, we thought at the start that there would be a higher yield of them – that perhaps 25% of the project's participants would join the accreditation paths. The actual figure was 20%. Possible reasons for this are reviewed in Chapter 6, but our concern now is to draw some practical insights, or lessons, from our own experience with the accreditation arrangements. The particular accreditation arrangements we made had to be negotiated with the university authorities, not just to ensure that standards were maintained but also to ensure transparency in this. The criteria that made these standards explicit were explained and explored with all participants in the accreditation paths. (They are contained in Appendix 6 and Appendix 7). It became clear that some teachers found the criteria a bit daunting. This was not because they were too academic; in fact the criteria are searchingly practical. Rather, the prospect of producing written assignments of 6,000 words was forbidding to many, not to speak of the 30,000 word requirement for an M.Ed. thesis. While acknowledging teachers' concerns here, the fact remains that university accreditation involves students in scholarly disciplines that include serious and sustained reading, and the production of significant quantities of writing.

Our experience with the accreditation aspect of the project highlights the desirability of non-university as well as university forms of accreditation for CPD activities. University forms of accreditation continue to expand and are marked by increasing degrees of flexibility. Non university forms of accreditation for most professions are characteristically designed and overseen by the relevant professional bodies, and in the case of teaching, by statutory Teaching Councils. In Scotland, the General Teaching Council has made much headway in devising a framework for professional development includes the pioneering programme for Chartered Teacher. The non-university route to Chartered Teacher involves portfolios and short reports rather than longer assignments and dissertations. As we concluded in Chapter 6, there is much to be learned from the Scottish example and that of teaching Councils in other countries. It is likely that work on the development of an Irish framework will commence soon under the auspices of the Teaching Council / An Comhairle Mhúinteoireachta. This provides a historic opportunity to match new professional prospects to Ireland's more distinctive strengths and traditions in teaching.

9. ICT in teaching and learning

At different points in this report we have commented on the different reactions to using ICT in teaching and learning that we encountered in the early days of the project. These ranged from the palpable enthusiasm of some, to the indifference or lack of awareness of others, to the techno-wariness of others still. In some schools dramatic developments in attitudes and practices took place. These were invariably associated with decisive actions taken by school leaders to avail of the project's resources to cultivate teachers' capacities, chiefly in ways that solved practical difficulties for them in particular aspects of their teaching. In other schools the momentum was slower, but in such cases progress became steady when the initial inroads were made and teachers showed an unforced, but increasing interest in becoming at home with more ICT resources. The positive responses of students to new features in teachers' approaches were instrumental in prompting such developments.

There still remains a minority of teachers, though clearly a diminishing one, who are indifferent or resistant to incorporating ICT in their work. The quickening pace of developments in ICT however, and especially pedagogical applications of ICT, is now bringing pressures that were barely evident when the TL21 project commenced. For instance, students who have experienced learning with interactive white boards in primary schools now expect the same in post-primary schools. Similarly, post-primary students who have taken warmly to their experiences with one teacher who uses ICT resources imaginatively and to good effect, want other teachers to do the same. Or teachers who were once comfortably within the ranks of the techno-wary or even the techno-phobic, discover that such ranks have depleted dramatically and that they are no longer such comfortable places. to be.

At school leadership level, Principals and Deputies are regularly hearing from colleagues about moves that are afoot in their schools to provide high quality electronic learning facilities Other school leaders who introduced ICT facilities to classrooms primarily for administrative and student record purposes are now discovering the more creative pedagogical possibilities of such resources. These are frequently pointed out by teachers who have become proficient and confident in pedagogical uses of ICT; sufficiently so as to be spontaneously on the scent of new possibilities.

We will conclude with brief comments on two ICT issues that gave rise to much debate and sometimes considerable disquiet in schools over the duration of the project. The first of these is the reliability of equipment. Teachers' views on this show strong unanimity: Where reliable ICT facilities can greatly enhance the experience of learning, unreliable equipment is not neutral, but a positive harm. The strong frustrations that account for such views arise from experiences where much imaginative lesson planning came to nought on a big occasion like a double period in a computer room, or where the attentions of students went noisily elsewhere while teachers spent up to ten minutes trying to fix an unexpected problem. Secondly, while 'territorial' issues affecting access to and the use of computer rooms in schools are still a cause for concern, the balance of work with ICT in teaching seems to be moving progressively to teachers' own classrooms. These are increasingly being furnished with electronic resources, including data projectors and networked computers; or quite often a data projector on a trolley is shared by two or three adjacent classrooms. The inherent logic of developments like these is that in Irish classrooms of the not too distant future such equipment, if not interactive whiteboards will be seen as standard equipment.

In case it is thought that this amounts to a recommendation to displace the teacher, we will leave the last word to the teacher whose remark we have quoted already as speaking for the majority of teachers with whom we worked on the TL21 project. 'ICT is a tool, not a panacea. It can assist and enhance the learning experience, it cannot teach. Its use must constitute a component of some lessons. The facilities must be classroom-based and available to the teacher as and when she requires to use them'.

Appendix 1

Participating Schools

St Joseph's Secondary School, Rochfortbridge, Co. Westmeath

Sacred Heart Secondary School, Tullamore, Co. Offaly

Mountmellick Community School, Mountmellick , Co. Laois

Heywood Community School, Ballinakill, Co Laois

Castlecomer Community School, Castlecomer, Co. Kilkenny

Scoil Dara, Kilcock, Co. Kildare

Maynooth Post-primary School, Maynooth Co. Kildare

Coláiste Chiaráin, Leixlip, Co. Kildare

Lucan Community College, Lucan, Co. Dublin

St. Peter's College, Dunboyne, Co. Meath

Ballinteer Community School, Ballinteer, Dublin 16

St Louis High School, Rathmines, Dublin 6

Christian Brothers' Secondary School, Synge St., Dublin 8

Loreto College, Crumlin, Dublin 12

St Paul's Secondary School, Greenhills, Dublin 12

Appendix 2

Members of the TL21 Project Team, Education Department NUI Maynooth, 2003-2007

Dr. Pádraig Hogan   (Team Leader)

Ms. Bernadette de Róiste

Mr. Gerry Jeffers (2004-2006)

Ms. Paula Kinnarney (2004-2005)

Mr. Alec MacAlister

Ms. Claire McAvinia (2004--2005)

Mr. Anthony Malone (2003-2006)

Dr. Rose Malone (on leave of absence 2004-05)

Dr. Aidan Mulkeen (on leave of absence 2004-present)

Ms. Geraldine Mooney Simmie (until October 2004)

Mr. Nigel Quirke-Bolt (since September 2005)

Mr. Greg Smith (since September 2005)

Part-time members :

Ms. Rose Dolan (November 2003-June 2004)

Ms. Diane Birnie (November 2003-June 2004)

Mr. Ciarán O'Sullivan (November 2003-June 2004)

Ms. Majella Dempsey (November 2004-June 2005)

Dr. Michael Quane (November 2004-June 2005)

Mr. Greg Smith (November 2004-June 2005)

Project Administrator:

Ms. Lilly Fahy

Appendix 3

Members of the National Advisory Committee

Professor John Coolahan (Chair)	Professor Emeritus, NUI Maynooth
Dr. Anne Looney,	Chief Executive, National Council for Curriculum and Assessment
Dr. Séamus McGuinness	School of Education, Trinity College, Dublin
Professor Gary Granville	Faculty of Education, National College of Art and Design, Dublin
Ms. Emer Egan	Assistant Chief Inspector, Department of Education and Science
Dr. Mark Glynn	Irish Pharmaceutical & Manufacturing Federation.
Ms. Mary Mc Glynn	Director, National Association of Principals and Deputy Principals

Appendix 4

Members of the International Consultative Panel

Professor Patrick Duignan Flagship for Educational Leadership, Australian Catholic University

Professor Michael Fullan Ontario Institute for Studies in Education, University of Toronto

Professor Louise Stoll International Congress for School Effective and Improvement

Dr. David Istance Centre for Educational Research and Innovation, OECD

Professor Malcolm Skilbeck Former Vice-Chancellor, Deakin University, Australia and former Deputy Director for Education, OECD

Dr. John Dallat Faculty of Education, University of Ulster, Jordanstown

Appendix 5

Example of a 'Rotation' Seminar

Ballybeg post-primary school has a teaching staff of fifty-two and four of these, Diarmuid, Gráinne, Peter and Heloise, have agreed to share with colleagues their experiences with specific pedagogical initiatives they have introduced in some of their classes. A one-day seminar is to be devoted to this purpose. At this seminar Gráinne will host a workshop on self-assessment and peer assessment by students. Diarmuid will host a workshop on the use of questioning to promote a more engaged kind of learning among students. Peter and Heloise will jointly host a workshop on the role of teachers' comments and feedback in the marking of students' work. Heloise uses comment-only marking, but Peter normally supplies marks as well as comments.

For the purposes of the seminar the staff is divided into three groups of seventeen, called groups A, B and C. The day is divided into three sessions of one-and-a-half hours each: Session 1 in the morning, Session 2 between morning break and lunch-time and Session 3 after lunch. There is a half-hour break between Session 1 and Session 2 and a one-hour break between Session 2 and Session 3. For Session 1, group A go to Gráinne's seminar, group B go to Diarmuid's and group C go to Heloise's and Peter's joint seminar. For session 2, Group C go to Gráinne's seminar, Group A go to Diarmuid's, and Group B go to the joint seminar. For Session 3, Group B go to Gráinne, Group C go to Diarmuid and Group A go to Heloise and Peter.

While such workshops are more informal than formal events, the presence of a chairperson in a low-profile way is helpful, chiefly for keeping an eye on time, but also to ensure if necessary that the workshop maintains a constructive dynamic. During each session the hosts give a succinct account of the initiatives they have been undertaking and highlight a number of issues for discussion, sometimes using short video clips if these are available. The bulk of the time in each session is taken up with such discussion. At the end of the day each staff member will have participated in three workshops and also in up to a further hour-an-a-half of discussion during the breaks. Disadvantages for the hosts are that they have to run the workshops three times and don't get an opportunity to go to the other workshops. Feedback from teachers who have hosted such workshops however is that the these disadvantages are far outweighed by the advantages. There is widespread agreement that the hosting of workshops, while it involves much painstaking preparation and leaves one tired at the end of the day, is a hugely affirming professional experience for teachers.

Appendix 6

Criteria for the Accreditation Pathways in the *TL21* Project

Version for Teacher Participants

These Criteria cover :
(A) The Preparatory Year Portfolio
(B) The H.Dip in Innovative Teaching and Learning
(C) The M.Ed in Innovative Teaching and Learning

Introductory Note: These criteria make frequent reference to the furnishing of evidence. As befits action research studies, such evidence can include various forms of record: e.g. documentation of critical friend contacts, of analyses by critical informants, of focus group meetings, of structured and semi-structured interviews, and of a range of triangulation strategies. Equally important, evidence of developments in professional practice can be well captured by other forms of record, such as audio or video recordings, or in a supplementary way by providing key samples of pedagogical resources (from learning games to ICT resources) that have been devised and used in these developments

(A) The Preparatory Year Portfolio must include analytic writing totalling 8,000 words, and relevant supporting materials: e.g., selected illustrative lesson plans and evaluations of their success, selected extracts from journals and from notes of critical friend meetings; pedagogical materials used, including video sequences, CDs, ICT materials etc..

The analytic writing in ___ portfolio must include:

- a coherent account of ___ making reference to difficulties in one's innovative practice, for dealing with them, and ___ encountered, strategies adopted ___ gains made;

- evidence of sustained critical reflection ___ one or more selected aspect(s) of one's own teaching;

94

- evidence of progressive engagement with one's critical friend and of the key benefits to one's teaching resulting from such engagement;

- evidence of regular use in classroom settings of ideas for innovative teaching and learning, such as those introduced and discussed in the workshops;

- evidence of a capacity to pursue independent research on one's practice, availing of pertinent research sources in an initial but discerning way.

(B) The Practical Research Project for the Higher Diploma award must be 8,000 words in length, and must be supported by relevant appendices and any other pertinent resources used.

The Practical Research Project must include evidence at a more advanced level of the features required in the Preparatory Year Portfolio. In addition it must include:

- evidence of working closely with colleagues beyond one's critical friend, and of the benefits such actions have sought and have actually accomplished.

- evidence of a creative use of a range of innovative resources in one's teaching and in one's pedagogical thinking and planning (e.g. technologies that could include conventional or digital projection, television/video, relevant software, other computer and/or web-based resources.)

- evidence of the kinds of gains made in pupils' learning as a consequence of the systematic use of innovative approaches.

- evidence of independent research capability, including appropriate reading: drawing perceptively on an appropriate range of research sources for a project of this scope.

(C) The M.Ed. dissertation should be 30,000 words in length. In certain circumstances a shorter dissertation may be acceptable, provided the dissertation is accompanied by an appropriate range of innovative pedagogical resources devised and produced by the candidate.

The M.Ed. dissertation should include, at a high level of proficiency, the features required in the Preparatory Year Portfolio and in the Practical Research Project. In addition it should include:

- evidence of an important initiative, or series of initiatives, that have been taken or are under way, to influence the wider learning environment of the school;

- evidence of a critical engagement with issues quality in learning, particularly as these feature in the school's development planning;

- evidence that students have, in a sustained way, become proficient in taking and active hand in their own learning, and of contributing in creative ways to the learning environment(s) of the school.

- evidence of promising, substantial ideas for good practice that have been tested and critically monitored in action and that are capable of being worthily recommended to a range of post-primary learning environments (and to the DES).

Appendix 7

Criteria for the Accreditation Pathways in the *TL21* Project

Version for Principals and Deputy Principals

Criteria for:
- **(A) Preparatory year Portfolio**
- **(B) H.Dip. in Innovative Teaching and Learning**
- **(C) M.Ed. in Innovative Teaching and Learning**

(A) The Preparatory Year Portfolio must include analytic writing totalling 8,000 words, and relevant supporting materials: e.g, selected parts of development plans and evaluations of their success, selected extracts from logs and from notes of critical friend meetings; innovative materials used : video sequences, CDs, ICT materials etc.

The analytic writing in the portfolio must include:

- a coherent account of important developments that have been initiated by the school leadership, making reference to difficulties encountered, strategies adopted for dealing with them, and significant gains made;

- evidence of sustained critical reflection on one or more selected aspect(s) of the school's leadership that are focused on teaching and learning issues;

- evidence of progressive engagement with professional colleagues, showing leadership on teaching and learning issues, and of benefits resulting from such engagement;

- evidence of use in one's own leadership practice of ideas such as those introduced and discussed in the seminars for Principals and Deputy Principals;

- evidence of a capacity to pursue independent research on one's practice, availing of pertinent research sources in an initial but discerning way.

(B) The Practical Research Project for the Higher Diploma award must be 8,000 words in length, and must be supported by relevant appendices and any other pertinent resources used.

The Practical Research Project must include evidence at a more advanced level of the features required in the Preparatory Year Portfolio. In addition it must include:

- evidence of working closely with colleagues beyond one's critical friend as Principal or Deputy Principal, and of the benefits such actions have sought and have actually accomplished.

- evidence of the kinds of gains made in the school's learning environment as a consequence of the systematic use of innovative approaches.

- evidence of independent research capability, including appropriate reading, drawing perceptively on an appropriate range of research sources for a project of this scope.

(C) The M.Ed. dissertation should be 30,000 words in length. In certain circumstances a shorter dissertation may be acceptable, provided the dissertation is accompanied by an appropriate range of innovative pedagogical resources devised and produced by the candidate.

The M.Ed. dissertation should include evidence, at a high level of proficiency, the features required in the Preparatory Year Portfolio and in the Practical Research Project. In addition it should include:

- evidence of an important initiative, or series of initiatives, that have been taken or are under way, to influence the wider learning environment of the school;

- evidence of a critical engagement with issues quality in learning, particularly as these feature in the school's development planning;

- evidence that students have, in a sustained way, become proficient in taking and active hand in their own learning, and of contributing in creative ways to the learning environment(s) of the school.

- evidence of promising, substantial ideas for good practice that have been tested and critically monitored in action and that are capable of being worthily recommended to a range of post-primary learning environments (and to the DES).

Appendix 8

Features of workshops in the TL21 project

Active participation:
The workshops were designed and convened by members of the TL21 project team, but from the start they were of an interactive nature, with lecture-style presentations being kept to the minimum. As mutual trust and openness grew among participants, participants themselves took a hand in the design of the workshops.

Clearly defined tasks:
These tasks arose from the specific workshop theme or themes), and were of two kinds: a) tasks to be carried out during the workshop; b) tasks to be carried out by participants between one workshop and the next.

Purposeful collaboration:
Participants came to engage in frank exchanges on their ideas and practices, and in particular on the initiatives they were working on in their own schools. This strengthened a sense of mutual support and of a shared responsibility for promoting high-quality learning.

Continuity:
The workshops were planned as scheduled events within a developmental sequence. As distinct from being 'once-off' events carried out at periodic intervals, each workshop had particular contributions to make to the progressive development of specific capacities on the part of the participants.

Feedback:
This included a) feedback evaluation) to the workshop convenor after each workshop and b)feedback progress reports) by participants to workshop colleagues *during* the workshop on teaching and learning initiatives being undertaken by participants in their own schools.

Emergent learning communities:
Features such as the five above cultivated mutual trust and openness among the workshop participants, leading to significant advances in participants' sense of professional identity and to a new awareness of such groupings as learning communities in which practitioners had a decisive sense of ownership.

BIBLIOGRAPHY

Black, P. & Wiliam, D. (1998) 'Inside the Black Box' at http://www.pdkintl.org/kappan/kbla9810.htm

Costa, A. & Kallick, B. 'Through the Lens of a Critical friend', *Educational Leadership*, October, 1993, (51), p.50.

Darling-Hammond, L.. (1995) *The Work of Restructuring Schools: Building from the Ground Up.* (New York, Teachers College Press).

European Commission (1996) *Teaching and Learning – Towards the Learning Society: White Paper on Education and Training* (Brussels, European Commission)

European Commission (2005), *Common European Principles for Teacher Competences and Qualifications.* (Brussels, European Commission)

Department of Education and Science (2005) *Chief Inspector's Report 2001-2004* (Dublin, Stationery Office)

Duignan, P. (2007) *Educational Leadership, Key Challenges and Ethical Tensions* (Melbourne, Cambridge University Press)

ESAI (1992) *Register of Theses on Educational Topics in Universities in Ireland,* Vol. 2, 1980-1990 (Dublin, Educational Studies Association of Ireland)

Fullan, M. (2003) *The Moral Imperative of School Leadership* (Thousand Oaks, California, Corwin Press)

Fullan, M. (2006) *Quality Leadership – Quality Learning: Proof Beyond Reasonable Doubt* (Cork, Lionra).

Coolahan, J. (2003) *Teachers Matter: Country Background Report for Ireland* (Dublin, The Stationery Office)

General Teaching Council for Scotland (2003) , *Guidelines for the Accreditation of Programmes Leading to the Award of Chartered Teacher* (at www.gtcs.org.uk)

Government of Ireland (1998) *Education Act* (Dublin, The Stationery Office)

Government of Ireland (2001) *Teaching Council Act* (Dublin, The Stationery Office)

Government of Ireland (2007) *National Development Plan 2007-2013: Transforming Ireland A Better Quality of Life for All* (Dublin, The Stationery Office)

Granville, G. (2005) *Cultivating Professional Growth: An Emergent Approach to Teacher Development.* (Dublin, Second Level Support Service)

IUA (2005) *Reform of 3ᵈ Level and Creation of 4ᵗʰ Level: Securing Competitive Advantage in the 21ˢᵗ Century* (Dublin, Irish Universities Association)

Leader, D. & Boldt, S. (1994), *Principals and Principalship: A Study of Principals in Voluntary Secondary Schools* (Dublin, Marino Institute of Education)

Lieberman, A. & Miller, L... (2004) *Teacher Leadership,* (San Francisco, Jossey-Bass)

Leithwood, K. (2005) *Teacher Working Conditions that Matter: A Synthesis of Evidence,* p.53.

MacBeath, J. (2006) *School Inspection and Self-evaluation: working with the New Relationship* (London, RoutledgeFalmer)

McLaughlin, M. W., & Talbert, J. E. (1993). *Contexts that Matter for Teaching and Learning: Strategic Opportunities for Meeting the Nation's Educational Goals.* (Stanford, CA: Stanford University, Center for Research on the Context of Secondary School Teaching)

Mc Manamly, S. (2002) *Providing for the Professional Development of Teachers in Second Level Schools* (Dublin, Second Level Support Service)

Morgan, M. Flanagan, R.   Kellaghan, T. (2001) *A Study of Non-Completion Rates in Undergraduate University Courses* (Dublin, Higher Education Authority, 2001)

OECD (2003) *Education at a Glance 2003* (Paris, OECD, 2003)

OECD (2005) *Teachers Matter: Attracting, Developing and Retaining Effective Teachers* (Paris, OECD)

OECD (2006) *Education at a Glance 2006* (Paris, OECD, 2006)

OECD (2007) *Education at a Glance 2007* (Paris, OECD, 2007)

Rose, J.   Reynolds, D.(2006) 'Teachers' Continuing Professional Development: A New Approach', paper presented at 20th Annual World International Congress for School Effectiveness and Improvement.

Schon, Donald A. (1982) *The Reflective Practitioner: How Professionals Think in Action* (New York, Basic Books)

Sergiovanni, T. (1992) *Moral leadership: Getting to the Heart of School Reform* (San Francisco, Jossey-Bass).

Shulman, L. in Lyons, N. (ed.) (1998) *With Portfolio in Hand* (New York, Teachers Colleges Press).

Starratt, R.J. (2004) *Ethical Leadership* (San Francisco, Jossey-Bass)

Stoll, L. Fink, D.   Earl. L. (2003) *It's About Learning (and it's about time)* (London, Routledge, 2003)

Sykes, G. (1996) 'Reform of and as Professional Development', *Phi Delta Kappan,* 77(7), 465-476.

Wenger, E. (1998) *Communities of Practice: Learning, Meaning, and Identity* (Cambridge, Cambridge University Press)